Chefs' Specials of California

Signature Dishes and Favorite Recipes
from Celebrated Chefs and Restaurants

ISBN 0-9787039-0-1

Printed in the United States of America.

Front Cover: Dungeness Crab Salad with Peas, Mint and Meyer Lemon Vinaigrette, Grace Restaurant, page 68.

Reed Exhibitions
383 Main Avenue
Norwalk, Connecticut 06851
www.reedexpo.com

Chefs' Specials of California can be purchased for business or promotional purposes. For more information, please contact:
Reed Exhibitions / Western Foodservice & Hospitality Expo
383 Main Ave, Norwalk, CT 06852
(203) 840-5612
www.chefsspecialscookbook.com

CALIFORNIA

Restaurant

ASSOCIATION

CELEBRATING 100 YEARS OF SERVICE
1906-2006

Thank you for picking up a copy of the *Chefs' Specials of California: Signature Dishes and Favorite Recipes from Celebrated Chefs and Restaurants* cookbook. Inside you will find some of the best recipes from restaurants and chefs across the Golden State, including some of the California Restaurant Association's 22,000 members. This cookbook celebrates California as one of the nation's premier eatery areas with a wide array of dishes from the state's top chefs and distinguished restaurants.

The California Restaurant Association and its Educational Foundation would like to thank all of those involved in putting this cookbook together in honor of the Association's 100 years of service and for donating a portion of the proceeds from the sale of this cookbook to the Educational Foundation's scholarship program.

The California Restaurant Association Educational Foundation (CRAEF) was founded in 1981 to increase the relevancy and effectiveness of educational preparation for hospitality careers and to encourage young men and women to pursue such careers. CRAEF provides educational seminars and mentoring opportunities for California Restaurant Association members, as well as internship opportunities, scholarships, and mentoring to those preparing for a career in our industry.

Each year, CRAEF awards scholarships to students pursuing post-secondary education in the foodservice industry. Since its inception, CRAEF has awarded nearly $700,000 in scholarships and grants to hospitality students and educators. CRAEF has launched a perpetual scholarship campaign to significantly increase the financial assistance available to the future leadership of California's foodservice industry.

For the restaurant and hospitality industry to fulfill its enormous potential growth, it is imperative that we attract a continuous supply of motivated, trained, and qualified men and women to professional foodservice careers. CRAEF believes that education is the key to satisfying the industry's need for career-minded individuals.

Thank you again for supporting CRAEF and making the future possible for students seeking careers as industry professionals. Happy cooking.

Sincerely,

Jot Condie
President and Chief Executive Officer
California Restaurant Association
1011 10th Street
Sacramento, California 95814
www.calrest.org

Table of Contents

(alphabetical by restaurant)

561 Restaurant

561 East Green Street
Pasadena, California 91206
626-405-1561
www.561restaurant.com

Lobster Roll Revisited
Lobster Salad with Preserved Lemons and Chives,
Grilled Brioche Bread, Baby Red Oak;
Citrus Jus "Shooter" with "Sweet Tart" Dust;
Truffled Potato Chips

By Chef Eric Osley

Serves 4

INGREDIENTS

Lobster Roll:
4 large slices brioche (with crust removed)
8 oz lobster salad (2 oz per portion) (see recipe below)
Baby red oak lettuce
1 oz premium olive oil to dress the red oak
1 oz citrus juice (in a rimmed shot glass, per portion)
1/4 tsp sweet tart dust (see recipe below)
1 handful truffled fingerling potato chips per portion (see recipe below)
Chervil for garnish

Lobster Salad:
1/2 lb fully cooked lobster meat or 1 (2-1/2 lb) live lobster
1/2 medium cucumber, peeled, seeded and finely diced
1/4 cup mayonnaise
1/2 Tbs fresh tarragon
2 small scallions, thinly sliced
2 oz chopped chives
1 Tbs finely minced preserved lemons (you can find at specialty stores or middle eastern markets)
Sea salt and freshly ground pepper, to taste

Dust:
Zest of 2 oranges
Zest of 2 lemons
Zest of 2 grapefruits
Zest of 2 limes
1/2 cup sugar
2 Tbs citric acid

Potato Chips:
3/4 lb fingerling potatoes (scrubbed well and dried)
4 cups vegetable oil, for frying
1/4 cup grated Parmesan
1 Tbs truffle oil
1 Tbs tarragon, chopped
1 tsp kosher salt
1 tsp freshly ground black pepper

PREPARATION INSTRUCTIONS

Lobster Salad: Boil the lobster in a simple court bouillon for about 4 minutes and shock immediately. Chop the lobster meat into large dice chunks. Add rest of ingredients into a bowl and bind with the mayo. Season. Taste to adjust any seasoning.

Citrus Juice: Combine the juice of 2 each oranges, grapefruits, lemons and limes and adjust with honey.

Dust: Toast the zest in a low oven. When dry add the sugar and zest to a robot coupe and combine. Add the citric acid and whisk completely.

Potato Chips: Using a mandoline, slice potatoes into slices as thin as possible and place in a large bowl of water to prevent discoloration. Heat oil in a large pot to 350°F. Pat potatoes completely dry. Add to oil in parts and cook until golden brown, stirring with a long handed spoon or "spider" to cook evenly, about 1-1/2 minutes. Drain on paper towels and place in a large bowl. Toss with the cheese, truffle oil, tarragon, salt, and pepper. Serve immediately.

(cont'd)

ABOUT THE CHEF

Chef Eric Osley is a graduate of the California School of Culinary Arts and the Sushi Chef Institute in Little Tokyo. Chef Osley worked for Spago's and Traxx in Los Angeles and Piccolo and Second Street Jazz Kitchen in Eugene, Oregon, before helping to open 561 Restaurant in 2000. Chef Osley has worked with top chefs such as Alice Waters and Jacques Pepin and has won several medals from the ACF. He was named a "Star Chef" in 2004 by Rosemary's Children Services Foundation.

SUGGESTED WINE PAIRING

- 2004 Cakebread Cellars Sauvignon Blanc, Napa Valley

THE STORY BEHIND THE RECIPE

I love this dish because it is a playful retake on a classic sandwich. As a chef it is always fun to take comfort food or items you grew up eating and transform them into something exciting and dynamic.

PREPARATION INSTRUCTIONS
(cont'd)

Presentation: Grill brioche bread. Place a heaping amount of lobster salad on brioche and top with dressed red oak. Dip rim of a shot glass into citrus juice and then into tart dust. Fill shot glass with citrus juice. Fry potatoes and season with chip seasoning. On a long rectangular plate, place open faced lobster sandwich on left, potato chips, and shot glass with a piece of chervil draped over top of glass. Garnish the plate with more chervil.

HELPFUL HINTS, VARIATIONS OR OTHER ADVICE

This cool appetizer could be used with Dungeness crab or poached Santa Barbara spotted prawns, when available. Play around with the citrus ratio and see how different levels of acidity will affect both the lobster roll and the wine. Try with preserved tangerines instead of preserved lemons.

The Admiral Risty

31250 Palos Verdes Drive West
Rancho Palos Verdes, California 90275
310-377-0050
www.admiral-risty.com

Roasted Red Peppers with Chicken & Hominy

By Chef Demetrius Crawford

Serves 10

INGREDIENTS

3 28-oz cans roasted red peppers
4 cups celery, medium dice
4 cups yellow onion, medium dice
3 Tbs garlic, medium dice
2-1/2 lbs chicken tenders, medium dice
1 28-oz can hominy
1 28-oz can diced red peppers
1 28-oz can corn kernels

1 Tbs dried sweet basil
1 tsp coarse salt
1 tsp coarse black pepper
5 whole dried bay leaves

Garnish:
1 cup sour cream
10 sprigs cilantro

PREPARATION INSTRUCTIONS

In steam kettle or large stock pot add roasted red peppers with their juice, celery, onions and garlic. Cook until tender. Using a robo mixer, purée until smooth (mixture will be a little gritty). This will give the soup some body. Add the remaining ingredients, simmer for 30 minutes. Serve right out of the pot, or chill and re-heat for the next day. Garnish with a teaspoon of sour cream and a sprig of cilantro.

HELPFUL HINTS, VARIATIONS OR OTHER ADVICE

I add 1/2 cup of uncooked white rice with the remaining ingredients. This gives the soup a little more body and makes it harder to scoop out all the goodies.

ABOUT THE CHEF

Chef Demetrius Crawford was raised in Seattle, WA where he graduated from Woodinville High School in 1989. While serving overseas in the Army, he picked up cooking under a colonel's direction. It was there that he began backpacking to Spain, Germany, Italy, Russia and France picking up various skills from local family cooks.

After leaving the Army with the love for cooking in his heart, Demetrius decided to attend culinary school at The Art Institute of Phoenix in Arizona. After five years as a sous chef, Demetrius found his home as Executive Chef for the Admiral Risty in Rancho Palos Verdes, CA where he has been cooking for the past two years. The "Risty" is a perfect match.

SUGGESTED WINE PAIRING

- 1999 McIlroy Cellars Syrah, Sonoma County

THE STORY BEHIND THE RECIPE

I ordered a case of red diced peppers and instead I received a case of roasted red peppers (must have been my one off day). I had to use them, so I made a soup. Hope you enjoy this comfort soup as much as my guests do. Eat up!

Adobe El Restaurante

9700 North Torrey Pines Road
La Jolla, California 92037
858-964-6505
www.estancialajolla.com

Ahi Tuna "Marmitako"

By Chef Jesse Frost

Serves 4

INGREDIENTS

1 lb fresh Ahi tuna loin, cut into large cubes
1/4 cup olive oil
1 onion, small dice
2 oz garlic
1 potato, small dice
4 ripe tomatoes, small dice
4 red peppers, small dice
1 tsp cayenne pepper

1 bay leaf
2 cups white wine
2 cups fish broth
Sea salt, fresh ground pepper

Garnish:
1 tsp capers
2 Tbs fresh parsley

PREPARATION INSTRUCTIONS

Heat olive oil in large earthenware pot. Sauté onions and garlic on low heat until tender. Add potatoes, tomatoes, peppers, cayenne and bay leaf. Season with sea salt and fresh pepper. Deglaze with white wine and reduce, then add fish broth. Simmer slowly for one hour. In a separate pan season Ahi and sear on all sides, cooking for about 3-4 minutes (medium rare). Remove fish and place on top of fish stew. Garnish with fresh parsley and capers. Serve from the earthenware pot with crisp Spanish white wine and crunchy bread.

HELPFUL HINTS, VARIATIONS OR OTHER ADVICE

You can substitute diver scallops for the Ahi tuna.

ABOUT THE CHEF

Having grown up in Mexico City and studied in Spain, Jesse Frost accentuates the Coastal Californian style of Adobe El Restaurante with a touch of Mexican and Spanish flare. He has also incorporated the creative expertise he developed while working in France. The dishes feature a melting pot of different tastes, fresh produce and bold flavors that produce exotic combinations and result in a "WOW" experience. Chef Frost also brings the "chef's farmers market" concept to Estancia La Jolla Hotel & Spa, which supports small farms that specialize in certain produce, rather than big corporations that conduct mass production. The result is what Chef Frost describes as comfort foods with a surprise twist - eclectic yet familiar, accessible yet refined. "The food will have more organic products and have a lot of thought put into it," says Chef Frost. Prior to joining Estancia La Jolla Hotel & Spa, Chef Frost served as Chef de Cuisine at the Prince of Wales in the Hotel Del Coronado in Coronado, California. Prior to this he gained experience as the Sous Chef for El Bizcocho at the Rancho Bernardo Inn and as the Chef De Partie at the Fairbanks Ranch Country Club. Chef Frost first started to hone his culinary skills at the California Culinary Academy, where he graduated with honors. After graduating, the chef worked for 4 years in the Bay Area at the restaurants La Folie and Firefly and, at the age of 24, was the opening chef for Bistro Chapeau. Chef Frost also worked as an apprentice in the 2-star Michelin restaurants Le Auberge Du Templiers in France and at the 3-star restaurants Martin Berasategui in San Sebastian, Spain. He was recently named a finalist for Best Chef of San Diego 2006 by the California Restaurant Association.

SUGGESTED WINE PAIRING

- Sauvignon Blanc, Spain

THE STORY BEHIND THE RECIPE

This is a signature dish in the restaurant. It derives its name from the earthenware pot called "marmita" and has a Basque origin.

Aliso Viejo Golf Club

25002 Golf Drive
Aliso Viejo, California 92656
949-598-9200/216
www.alisogolf.com

Barbecue Chicken Wrap

By Chef Cyndy Klein

Serves 1

INGREDIENTS

5 oz boneless, skinless, grilled chicken breast
2 oz barbecue sauce
1 cup shredded romaine lettuce
1 oz corn kernels

1 oz tomato, chopped
1 oz pepper jack cheese, shredded
2 oz ranch dressing
1 large flour tortilla

PREPARATION INSTRUCTIONS

Grill and dice chicken breast. Mix with heated barbecue sauce. Combine lettuce, corn, tomato, cheese and ranch dressing in a mixing bowl and toss. Heat flour tortilla and spread lettuce mixture on top. Place chicken over lettuce mixture and roll up tortilla burrito-style. Cut on diagonal and serve standing up. Accompany with your choice of side item.

ABOUT THE CHEF

Cyndy Klein is a graduate of CIA Hyde Park, NY, 1986. Cyndy has worked in fine dining, catering, retail deli, health care, hotels and as a personal chef. Her emphasis has always been on customer service and satisfaction, and the adaptability of menus to the client's specific needs. She has spent 20 years in Southern California, and is currently Executive Chef and F&B Manager at Aliso Viejo Golf Club.

SUGGESTED WINE PAIRING

- Chardonnay
- Sauvignon Blanc

THE STORY BEHIND THE RECIPE

Our clientele likes the ease of taking a wrap out on the course, so it was natural to put these potentially messy ingredients into a tidy package.

Ana Mandara

891 Beach Street
San Francisco, California 94109
415-771-6800
www.anamandara.com

Turbinado-Chili-Glazed Fresh-Water Prawns with Haricots Verts and White Peach

By Chef Khai Duong

Serves 4

INGREDIENTS

8 extra colossal (U/10 per lb) whole fresh water or tiger
  prawns with the heads and tails attached
4 to 5 Tbs vegetable oil
1 tsp garlic, finely minced
1/2 tsp chili powder
2 Tbs turbinado sugar or brown sugar
2 Tbs of the reserved prawn roe (optional)
4 Tbs white wine
3 Tbs Vietnamese fish sauce,
  or to taste

Haricots Verts and White Peach:

2 Tbs unsalted butter
4 oz haricots verts or Blue Lake green beans,
  trimmed and blanched
1 white peach or persimmon, peeled and julienned
  (1/8" thick by 1-1/2" long)
Pinch of kosher salt
Black pepper, to taste

PREPARATION INSTRUCTIONS

Shell and devein prawns, leaving head and tail intact. Remove roe from behind head and reserve. If using prawn roe, add 2 tablespoons of oil into a large skillet. Without the roe, use only 1 tablespoon oil. Add garlic to the oil and sauté over medium-high for about 15 seconds until a light golden color. Add the chili powder, sugar and, if available, prawn roe. Whisk together until thick and completely blended, about 30 seconds. Over high heat add the wine and whisk together for about 1 minute or until slightly thickened. Add the fish sauce and continue whisking until the mixture has reduced by half, about 1 to 2 minutes longer. The sauce should be a light creamy glaze consistency. Set aside. Keep warm.

In a separate large skillet, add 2 to 3 tablespoons of the remaining oil over medium-high heat. When hot, add prawns and toss occasionally, until lightly seared on all sides. Cook until medium-rare (feels firm to the touch when pressed). Remove prawns and pour all oil out of skillet. Return the prawns to the pan and pour the sauce on top. Cook together over medium-high heat until the sauce glazes the prawns. Keep warm.

Haricots Verts and White Peach:

In a skillet over medium heat, melt butter. When hot (but not burning), add haricots verts. Toss to cook and coat with butter, about 1 minute or until tender (but still crisp). Add peaches, salt and pepper; toss until mixed.

To Assemble:

Divide and arrange the beans and white peach in the center of 4 plates. Top each with two prawns. Pour extra sauce on top and on to the sides of the plates. Serve hot.

ABOUT THE CHEF

Using family recipes, Ana Mandara's Executive Chef Khai Duong has been at the forefront of introducing upscale Vietnamese cuisine to the American palate. He has created original modern Vietnamese cuisine through classic Vietnamese recipes using French technique and reflecting American style. Duong combines culinary inspiration from his native village of Nha Trang (on the south central coast of Vietnam) with world-class experience. Duong received a Grand Diploma, Summa Cum Laude, in Classical French Cuisine and Patisserie, and graduated first in his class at Le Cordon Bleu Academie Culinaire De Paris. He earned an Advanced Certificate from the École Lenotre Française Gastronomique in Paris and a Diploma of Connoisseur in Wine from the Academie Du Vin, also in Paris. Duong's professional experience includes the Maui Prince Hotel, the Boca Raton Resort Hotel, Le Bernardin in New York City and Le Colonial in Beverly Hills. Duong has appeared on the PBS television series Great Chefs of America; received the Great Chefs of New England Award from A & P International Foods, and assisted in a dinner at NYC's The Beard House. Chef Khai, 39 years old, is married with 2 young children, and travels frequently to keep his culinary horizons fresh.

HELPFUL HINTS, VARIATIONS OR OTHER ADVICE

In Vietnam, huge fresh-water prawns are common but expensive, primarily reserved for special occasions. If you are lucky enough to find them with the heads attached, they create quite a dramatic presentation. If fresh is not possible, try looking in the freezer section of an Asian market for these extra large whole prawns. If there is roe, that makes it even better. This recipe can be prepared without the roe; however, it is the secret ingredient that makes this sauce luxurious. Headless tiger prawns may be substituted and it is not necessary that they are the colossal size. To prevent overcooking, Chef Khai sautés the prawns and sauce in separate skillets, a technique he adopted from his French culinary training. After sautéing is finished and the sauce is made, the two skillets can be set aside until you are ready to finish the entrée. Just seconds before serving, turn the heat on under both skillets, toss the prawns with the hot glaze, and you are done.

SUGGESTED WINE PAIRING

• 2003 Dr. Loosen Riesling, Germany

THE STORY BEHIND THE RECIPE

Combining fruit with haricots verts was an accidental blessing. One afternoon Chef Khai noticed his daughter Aivy snacking on persimmon and green beans. Chef Khai was intrigued by this unusual combination and decided to try it as an accompaniment to this sweet, salty, and spicy prawn entrée. It worked. When persimmons are out of season, Chef Khai found that white peaches impart the same magic.

A'Roma Ristorante

30 Centerpointe Drive, Suite 1
La Palma, California 90623
714-523-3729
www.ferrarisaroma.com

Salmone al Forno

By Chef Gerardo Lopez

Serves 1

INGREDIENTS

8 oz salmon filet
1/4 cup sautéed spinach
2 Tbs Parmigiano cheese, grated
2 Tbs feta cheese
3 Tbs minced sautéed red bell pepper
1 Tbs butter, softened
White pepper and salt to taste

Creamy Roasted Red Bell Pepper Sauce:
1 Tbs butter
1 clove garlic, minced
1/4 cup purée of roasted red bell pepper
2 oz white wine
4 oz manufacturing cream
2 Tbs Parmigiano cheese, grated
Salt and white pepper, to taste

PREPARATION INSTRUCTIONS

Cut a pocket in salmon and stuff with mixture of spinach, Parmigiano cheese, feta cheese, minced red bell pepper and butter, seasoned to taste with salt and white pepper. Bake at 400°F for 6-8 minutes according to preference. Place salmon on a bed of creamy roasted red bell pepper sauce and top with same sauce.

Creamy Roasted Red Bell Pepper Sauce:

Sauté garlic in butter. Add purée of roasted red bell pepper, white wine, manufacturing cream and grated Parmigiano cheese. Sauté until sauce thickens. Add more butter if necessary.

HELPFUL HINTS, VARIATIONS OR OTHER ADVICE

Serves well with roasted rosemary potatoes and sautéed fresh asparagus. Salmon could be placed on a bed of risotto or rice pilaf in place of the roasted potatoes.

ABOUT THE CHEF

Gerardo Lopez is classically trained in French and Italian cooking. Gerardo has spent 13 years at A'roma Ristorante. He has had previous experience at L'Opera and Andiamo in Long Beach, CA.

SUGGESTED WINE PAIRING

• Canaletto Pinot Grigio

THE STORY BEHIND THE RECIPE

This dish was created by Gerardo Lopez from his extensive experience with seafood and sauces.

Asia Los Feliz
Neo Thai • Steak • Sushi

3179 Los Feliz Boulevard
Atwater Village, California 90039
323-906-9498
www.asialosfeliz.com

Lamb Chops with Spicy Mango and Avocado Sauce

By Chef Visanu Chivacharern

Serves 2

INGREDIENTS

Lamb:
1 small rack of lamb, frenched, approximately 1.25 lbs (7-8 bones)
1/4 lb seasoned steak fries
Frisée for garnish

Marinade:
1/4 cup fish sauce
1/4 cup oyster sauce
1/4 cup sugar
1 piece lemongrass, finely chopped
1 Tbs cilantro
1 tsp minced garlic
1/2 tsp white pepper
1/4 cup peanut oil

Mango Sauce:
1/4 cup fish sauce
1/4 cup lime juice
1/4 cup sugar
1 Tbs peanut oil
4 Thai chilis or Serrano chilis, thinly sliced
1 mango, cubed
1 avocado, cubed
2-3 cherry tomatoes

PREPARATION INSTRUCTIONS

Meat:
Cut lamb into 1- or 2-bone pieces (thinner pieces are less gamey). Mix marinade ingredients well. Add lamb pieces and marinate for 30 minutes.

Mango Sauce:
Mix fish sauce, lime juice, sugar, peanut oil and chilis together. Add mango and avocado. Before serving, split cherry tomatoes and add to sauce for garnish.

Cooking:
Place lamb pieces on grill over high heat. Cook to medium rare. Meanwhile, cook steak fries.

Plating:
Pile fries in the middle of the plate, then place the pieces of lamb around fries with bones pointed toward the center. Rub some sauce on lamb for additional flavor. Place frisée on top of bones. Drizzle mango sauce around plate.

HELPFUL HINTS, VARIATIONS OR OTHER ADVICE

You can substitute lemongrass oil for the fresh lemongrass. The oil will give you a better aroma and less work.
For lamb lovers, try cutting 2-bone piece instead of one. You will find it easier to produce a perfect med-rare.

ABOUT THE CHEF

Executive Chef Visanu decided to break away from the norm and create his own style of food. He called this new type of cuisine "Neo Thai." Taking a little bit from every cuisine including French, Italian, Chinese, Japanese, Thai, Classic American and American Southwest, Chef Visanu created a host of proprietary sauces that, combined with only the finest cuts of meat and the freshest fish and vegetables, developed into an absolutely unique taste experience. At the same time, he never lost sight of the importance of a healthy diet. Neo Thai recipes do not call for MSG, large amounts of starch or handfuls of salt.

SUGGESTED WINE PAIRING

- 2001 Domaine la Roquette Chateaneuf-Du-Pape Blanc
- 2002 Donum, Pinot Noir

THE STORY BEHIND THE RECIPE

This dish was actually created for my girlfriend, who does not like lamb. Lemongrass helped me hide the gaminess of the meat, and the sauce helps creates a unique lamb eating experience. At my restaurant, I sprinkle 20-year old balsamic vinegar around the plate to add to presentation and personally, I just love it with the fries.

Avenue X Restaurant

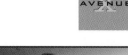

134 North Mill Street
Santa Paula, California 93060
805-933-3337
www.AvenueXRestaurant.com

Chinese Five-Spice Apple Phyllo Rolls with Buttered Walnut Ice Cream

By Chef Tiffany Buchanan

Serves 8 (2 rolls per serving)

INGREDIENTS

Phyllo Wrap:
12 sheets phyllo dough, thawed at room temperature
3 oz unsalted butter, melted
4 Tbs sugar

Chinese Five-Spice Apple Filling:
4 medium apples (Pink Lady or Granny Smith), peeled, cored and julienned. (They should look like french fry potatoes)
1/4 cup brown sugar
1 Tbs cornstarch

1 Tbs Chinese five-spice powder
Juice and zest of 1 lemon

Buttered Walnut Ice Cream:
1 qt homemade (or good quality store-bought) vanilla ice cream
4 oz unsalted butter
1/2 cup brown sugar
1 cup walnuts, toasted
1 tsp salt

PREPARATION INSTRUCTIONS

Phyllo Wrap and Filling: Preheat oven to 375°F. In a medium bowl toss together the apples, brown sugar, cornstarch, Chinese 5 spice powder, lemon zest and juice, and set aside. Lay the phyllo sheets on a clean work surface. Remove 1 sheet and lay it flat. Cover remaining phyllo with a kitchen towel. With a pastry brush, brush the single sheet with melted butter and then sprinkle with 2 tsp of the sugar. Lay a second sheet of phyllo on top of the first and again butter and sugar it. Continue in the same manner with a third sheet of phyllo. Cut phyllo vertically into 4 sections (you should end up with 4 long rectangles). Place roughly 1/4 of an apple on the short end of each rectangle and roll up the phyllo around the apples, tucking in the ends as you go. Repeat this process with the remaining phyllo sheets and apples. Place the rolls seam side down on parchment-lined baking sheet. Brush tops with remaining butter and sprinkle with sugar. Bake till golden brown and crispy, 18-25 minutes.

Ice Cream: In a non-stick sauce pan melt 4 oz unsalted butter. Add 1/2 cup brown sugar and stir till sugar has melted. Add toasted walnuts and salt, stirring till all the nuts have been coated. Turn out nuts onto a baking sheet and let cool. Chop nuts into small pieces. Soften ice cream and fold in nuts. Pour into an 8-inch square pan that has been lined with plastic wrap. Lay a piece of parchment directly on the surface of ice cream and freeze till hard.

Assembly: Turn out ice cream onto a cutting board. With a hot, dry knife cut into 8 squares. Place 1 square on a plate, lay one apple roll across the top. Cut the second apple roll in half diagonally and lean the pieces against the ice cream.

ABOUT THE CHEF

Tiffany Buchanan attended Parson's School of Design before figuring out that her true passion is desserts. Tiffany attended the California Culinary Academy in San Francisco to study baking and pastry. She worked as the Pastry Chef at the Coconut Grove (a three-star 1940's supper club), and went on to open Gracie's, in the theater district. Tiffany recently moved to Southern California, and is currently working for Chef Richard Hyman at Avenue X.

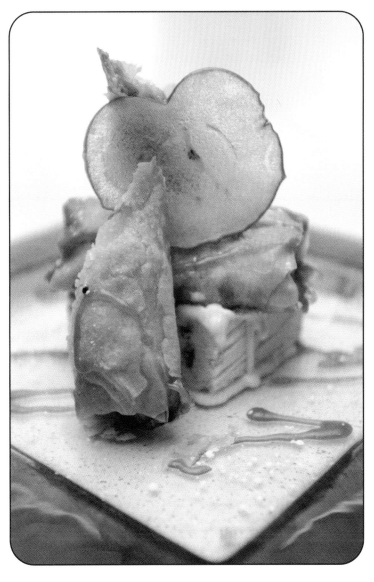

HELPFUL HINTS, VARIATIONS OR OTHER ADVICE

Apple rolls can be made ahead of time and stored in the freezer unbaked for up to 1 month. Ice cream can be made ahead and stored in the freezer. These can be embellished further with caramel sauce.

THE STORY BEHIND THE RECIPE

Many people love apple pie, and I was looking for a way to bring in all the flavors and textures of a pie in a non-traditional manner. While these take a little time to prepare, the fact that they can be made ahead of time and kept frozen is a real bonus. You will always be ready for those unexpected guests!

Azul La Jolla

1250 Prospect Street
La Jolla, California 92037
858-454-9616
www.azul-lajolla.com

Atlantic Sea Scallops "Green Eggs & Ham"

By Chef Orion Balliet

Serves 4

INGREDIENTS

- 8 (U/10) dry packed Atlantic sea scallops ("dry packed" means no TSP is used)
- 8 slices smoked bacon
- 2 tsp Granulated garlic
- 8 1/4-in slices brioche bread (egg and butter rich French bread)

Sauce:
- 3 red bell peppers
- 6 oz melted butter
- 1 chipotle pepper in adobo, canned
- 2 egg yolks
- Salt and pepper, to taste

Garnish:
- 2 Tbs wasabi tobiko (wasabi-flavored flying fish caviar)

PREPARATION INSTRUCTIONS

Wrap one slice of bacon around each scallop and season with granulated garlic, salt and pepper. Place in refrigerator until ready to cook. With a large round cutter (5" diameter), cut eight circle slices of brioche bread. With a smaller round cutter the same diameter as the scallops (2" diameter), cut out the center of each slice of bread. Toast bread until golden brown in a 350°F oven. After toasting, leave bread out at room temperature, uncovered.

Sauce:

Roast red bell peppers over open flame or in very hot oven at 500°F until peppers are soft and dark brown on the outside. Place peppers in a covered container and let sit on the counter for 10 minutes. While waiting for the peppers, melt butter on stove until bubbling, but do not let brown. Remove skin, seeds and stem from peppers and place in a food processor with chipotle pepper and egg yolks. Start to purée the peppers and yolks while slowly adding the hot melted butter to create an emulsion. Finish with salt and pepper, to taste. Strain through a very fine strainer. Keep sauce warm, above 140°F, until ready to use.

To prepare dish, sear scallops in a hot sauté pan with a small amount of oil. Roll scallops on side to make sure bacon becomes a nice dark brown color. Scallops should be cooked to an internal temperature of 130°F, which takes about 4-5 minutes.

Plating:

Place two pieces of round brioche toast on plate. Place scallops in cut-out centers and spoon sauce as desired. Garnish each scallop with wasabi tobiko on top.

ABOUT THE CHEF

Orion Balliet began his cooking career at the age of fourteen, working for a renowned French Master Chef. He spent the next few years studying the techniques of the old world, including the ideologies of Escoffier and Bocuse. It was their philosophies that influenced Orion's passion and vision for fine, beautiful, quality food. After his apprenticeship Orion found himself in San Francisco, at the California Culinary Academy. While in school, he earned the position of Sous Chef under the pioneer of California Cuisine, Mr. Jeremiah Tower, at Stars Restaurant. In 1994 Orion graduated on the dean's list and accepted his first Executive Chef position at the young age of twenty-one. Orion's travels have led him around the globe, studying the culinary traditions of Eastern and Western Europe and the southern Mediterranean. He has earned the position of Executive Chef in an exclusive four-star, four-diamond private club and most recently comes from a position at the admired Villagio Inn and Spa in the Napa Valley wine country in California. Since his first chef position, Orion has honed his management philosophy, building a team culture of employees. This team design uses entry level individuals who have proven their potential and desire to succeed. The team provides these aspiring chefs and restaurant professionals the opportunity to learn everything necessary to become an Executive Chef or Restaurant Manager with emphasis on individual empowerment. This atmosphere has been proven time and time again to produce a cohesive unit with high productivity, loyalty and creativity. The team does not accept mediocrity and has a competitive edge that keeps it in front of the competition. In return, the team provides the employer with a cost-effective workforce in today's tough economic environment.

Currently the Executive Chef of Azul la Jolla, Orion Balliet has mastered his specialty of California Cuisine and developed a new style he calls "California Spa Cuisine." This new technique uses California flavors with healthy concepts (no dairy, wheat or refined sugars). Evolving with the food he creates, Orion is always on the cutting edge of modern cooking.

THE STORY BEHIND THE RECIPE

This dish was created in homage to Dr. Theodor "Seuss" Geisel who resided in La Jolla, California. In 1960 he wrote the book "Green Eggs & Ham" as a bet with his publisher that he could not write a book with only fifty words.

Barona Oaks Steakhouse

1932 Wildcat Canyon Road
Lakeside, California 92040
619-443-2300
www.barona.com

....

Lobster "Mojito"

By Chef Dean Thomas

Serves 2

INGREDIENTS

Lobster:
6 oz cold-water Maine lobster tail, poached
1/2 cup Napa cabbage, very thinly shaved

"Mojito" Vinaigrette:
1 sugar cube per glass
1 oz aged golden rum
4 Mexican limes, juiced
1 tsp sherry vinegar

1 shallot, minced
1 tsp mint leaves, cut in thin ribbons
1/4 tsp sea salt
2 small ice cubes

Garnish:
2 wedges lavash cracker
2 lime slices, dried slowly with sugar in oven
Flat leaf parsley sprig for garnish

PREPARATION INSTRUCTIONS

Lobster:
Begin by poaching the lobster tail in court-bouillon and chill. In a large martini glass, place the shaved Napa cabbage and fan the poached lobster tail. Garnish with the lavash cracker, parsley and dried lime.

"Mojito" Vinaigrette:
Using a martini shaker, mix the vinaigrette ingredients, add the ice cubes and shake tableside with vigor. Pour "Mojito" vinaigrette over the lobster, flavoring the Napa cabbage into a slaw. Bon Appetite!

ABOUT THE CHEF

A native of the Midwest and the Chicago-land area, Dean Thomas began his career in the hospitality industry as a young dishwasher for an Italian chef who took Dean under his wing. Dean went to Joliet Junior College to study Culinary Arts and soon moved on to Hilton Head Island, South Carolina to gain experience at opening many of the plantation developments. Dean took a sabbatical in pastries working for Chef Kurt Buchi at the Intercontinental Resort, and soon became the Outlet Chef for the Carolina Café at the Westin Hilton Head 5-Diamond Resort.

Bistro K

1000 Fremont Avenue
South Pasadena, California 91030
626-799-5052
www.lqmanagementservices.com

Maple Leaf Duck Breast Salad with Confit Kumquats

By Chef Laurent Quenioux

Serves 6

INGREDIENTS

4 (4-oz) boned duck breast halves

Confit Kumquat:
1 cup kumquats, halved
8 oz chicken broth
2 Tbs sugar

Salad:
2 heads radicchio
2 bunches watercress

4 Belgian endives
1 cup sliced green onions

Dressing:
2 Tbs balsamic vinegar
4 Tbs extra virgin olive oil
1/4 tsp salt
1/8 tsp pepper
1/3 oz curry paste

1 shallot, minced
1 clove garlic, chopped

Garnish:
3 ripe avocados

PREPARATION INSTRUCTIONS

Duck:

Preheat oven to 450ºF. Place large nonstick skillet coated with cooking spray over medium-high heat until hot. Meanwhile, skin duck (face down). Cook 2 minutes on each side or until lightly browned. Place duck in an 11" X 7" baking dish coated with cooking spray. Bake at 450ºF for 20 minutes or until done (should be pink/medium rare). Let cool. Cut into 1/4" wide strips.

Confit Kumquat:

In a small pan combine kumquat halves with chicken broth and sugar. Cook until you have a thick syrup coating around the kumquats, then mix with duck.

Dressing:

Combine salt, pepper, balsamic vinegar, olive oil, curry paste, shallot and garlic in a small bowl. Stir well.
Keep 1/3 for tossing with lettuce.

Salad:

Peel and slice avocado halves to form a crown. In a bowl, mix leaves from radicchio, watercress and endive with green onions and 1/3 the dressing.

Plating:

Pour dressing over duck mixture and toss well. Serve salad in the avocado crown and add duck mixture on the top.

ABOUT THE CHEF

Laurent Quenioux's culinary skills were honed in France under renowned French chefs. Mr. Quenioux later moved to Los Angeles and opened The 7th Street Bistro in the heart of Downtown Los Angeles. The Bistro was voted for nine straight years one of the best restaurants in Los Angeles, and received many awards and favorable reviews. One of the reasons for this success was that Mr. Quenioux, who was both chef and owner, had his personal imprimatur on all things. His love of all things related to the service of food has allowed him to succeed in all his ventures.

SUGGESTED WINE PAIRING

- 2003 Les Tuffeaus Chenin Blanc, Montlouis-Sur-Loire

California School of Culinary Arts

California School of Culinary Arts
Le Cordon Bleu Program
Pasadena

521 East Green Street
Pasadena, California 91101
626-229-1300/1519
www.csca.edu

CALIFORNIA
Restaurant
ASSOCIATION
CELEBRATING 100 YEARS OF SERVICE
1906-2006

Alligator Filé Gumbo

By Chef Larry Bressler

Serves 6

INGREDIENTS

1 lb Andouille sausage,
  1/2" bias cut slices
2 oz olive oil
1/2 cup onion, small dice
3 cloves garlic, minced
1/2 cup red bell pepper, small dice
1/2 cup green bell pepper, small dice
1/2 cup celery, small dice
2 oz flour, toasted in a 300°F oven
  until light brown

3 Tbs filé powder
1 tsp tomato paste
1 tsp dried oregano
1 tsp dried thyme
2 Tbs fresh parsley, chopped
1 tsp cayenne pepper
1 tsp white pepper
1 tsp black pepper
1/2 gal chicken stock

1 lb alligator tail meat, cleaned of
  connective tissue, small dice
1 (28-oz) can whole tomatoes,
  slightly crushed
Hot pepper sauce and Worcestershire
  sauce, to taste
1-1/2 cups dry sherry
Salt, to taste

PREPARATION INSTRUCTIONS

Sauté Andouille slices in olive oil until lightly browned. Add onions, garlic, peppers and celery and sweat until vegetables are translucent. Add toasted flour, filé powder, tomato paste, herbs and dry seasonings. Stir to evenly coat vegetables and sausage. Add chicken stock, alligator meat, tomatoes, hot pepper sauce, Worcestershire, sherry and salt. Reduce heat and let the gumbo simmer for 1 to 1-1/2 hours. Add additional stock as needed to adjust the consistency of gumbo during cooking. Adjust seasonings to taste. Serve with steamed white or basmati rice, chopped parsley and bias cut scallions.

HELPFUL HINTS, VARIATIONS OR OTHER ADVICE

You can find alligator at 99 Ranch Market or source it through your seafood purveyor.

ABOUT THE CHEF

Larry Bressler graduated from The Culinary Institute of America, Hyde Park, New York in December, 1983. He earned his B.S. at Florida International University, School of Hotel & Restaurant Management, Miami, Florida in May, 1987. Chef Larry started in the restaurant business at age 13 as a dishwasher for a Chinese restaurant owned by a family friend. He worked in a management training program (Distributive Education Clubs of America) during high school and won first place in the state of Illinois for Restaurant Management Technology in 1981. Bressler also worked as a Banquet Supervisor on the opening crew for The Windsor Court Hotel in New Orleans during the World's Fair in 1984–1985; at the Mayfair House Hotel in Coconut Grove, FL, a five star/five diamond property, as a Saucier from 1985 to 1987; and at Mustard's Grill in Yountville, CA as a Sous Chef for Napa Valley celebrity chef Cindy Pawlcyn from 1987 to 1989. In addition, Chef Larry was the owner and head chef of Gerard's French Restaurant, a 50-seat French Bistro in Riverside, CA from 1997 to 2003. He is a chef instructor at the California School of Culinary Arts, Pasadena, CA where he is imparting close to thirty years of industry experience to the future chefs, pastry chefs and restaurant managers.

SUGGESTED WINE PAIRING

• 2005 Firestone Gewurztraminer

THE STORY BEHIND THE RECIPE

I am a huge fan of New Orleans, having worked there in 1984 and 1985 during the World's Fair. This soup was created as part of a tasting menu for a fundraiser for Dine for America, for which I coordinated efforts at the California School of Culinary Arts, Pasadena, Le Cordon Bleu Program, last October. One hundred percent of the money raised from the event was donated to Hurricane Katrina relief. The three-soup course also included Oyster Rockefeller Bisque and Traditional Turtle Soup.

Casa Guadalajara

4105 Taylor Street
San Diego, California 92110
619-295-5111
www.casaguadalajara.com

CALIFORNIA
Restaurant
ASSOCIATION
CELEBRATING 100 YEARS OF SERVICE
1906-2006

MEXICAN
RESTAURANT

Pescado a la Naranja with Cilantro-Lime Coleslaw

By Chef Jose Duran

Serves 2

INGREDIENTS

Pescado a la Naranja:
1 clove garlic, chopped
1/4 cup lime juice
1 oz Maggi seasoning
Salt to taste
2 (8-oz) sea bass or cod fillets
1/4 stick butter
1/2 cup orange juice
1/3 cup stuffed green olives, sliced 1/4 inch thick
2 tsp fresh cilantro, finely chopped

Cilantro-Lime Coleslaw:
2 Tbs fresh lime juice
1 clove garlic, minced
2 Tbs fresh cilantro, finely chopped
Salt, to taste
1/2 tsp black pepper
Dash Worcestershire sauce
4 Tbs olive oil
2 cups red or mixed cabbage, chopped

PREPARATION INSTRUCTIONS

Pescado a la Naranja:
Combine garlic, lime juice, Maggi seasoning and salt in a nonreactive bowl. Add fish and marinate 20 minutes. Grill fish 2 1/2 to 3 minutes per side. Use fork to peek inside to see if flesh is opaque. In a skillet, melt butter and add orange juice and olives. Cook sauce until it thickens and turns a slight caramel color. Add chopped cilantro to sauce. Place fish on a plate and top with sauce. Serve with Cilantro-Lime Coleslaw.

Cilantro-Lime Coleslaw:
Place all ingredients, except cabbage, in bowl and whisk together thoroughly. Add cabbage and toss to coat.

HELPFUL HINTS, VARIATIONS OR OTHER ADVICE

Maggi (MAH-jee) is commonly used in Latin America, Africa, Asia, and Europe. It was invented in Switzerland in the 1880s and was adopted by the French. It looks like soy sauce and contains hydrolyzed soy, but the taste is very different. Be careful, a little goes a long way. This dish serves very well with black beans.

ABOUT THE CHEF

As a boy, Jose Duran came to think of food in a spiritual light. "The chefs in Mexico City, where I was raised, were treated with the respect given to priests," he explains. "I was in awe of the chefs, and even though I just scrubbed the floors at first, they treated me with respect and dignity." At 16, Duran began working in a number of Mexico City restaurants where he learned Asian, Italian, Mexican and French cuisines. Perhaps the most important lessons were at VIP's, a successful chain of restaurants, where he learned business and management skills. He rose to Executive Chef, and in 1980 VIPs sent him to Los Angeles to open its first restaurant in the United States. The venture was foiled by a recession, but Duran began working at Mr. A's, a fine dining spot in San Diego. Three years later it was love at first sight when he visited Casa de Bandini in Old Town, an upscale Mexican restaurant owned by Diane Powers. He was soon working there as a sous chef, and eventually became Executive Chef. He had always wanted to own his own restaurant, and in 1986 he opened Guadalajara with high hopes and thin pockets. "It was in the east part of downtown, the rent was reasonable—because at the time it was pretty run-down and scary. I just couldn't get people to come to the area." In 1995 he learned Powers was opening another Old Town restaurant, Casa Guadalajara, and they reconnected. "She gave me everything I needed to succeed. All she asked was that I make consistently great food," he said. And that he did. The award-winning Casa Guadalajara is a destination restaurant for locals and world travelers alike. The traditional Mexican food infused with Italian and Asian flavors reflects Duran's culinary journey.

SUGGESTED WINE PAIRING

- 2004 Luna Vineyards Pinot Grigio
- A crisp Sauvignon Blanc
- A non-tannic red such as a Pinot Noir
- A light Merlot

(Wine recommendations by Ron James)

THE STORY BEHIND THE RECIPE

Pescado a la Naranja has its roots in the Mexico City kitchen of chef Duran's grandmother. "Her kitchen to me was almost a sacred space, with wondrous ingredients gracing almost every inch of it," says Duran. Chef Duran introduced Pescado a la Naranja at the International Seafood Cooking Competition in Ensenada, Mexico where it was awarded the top trophy as the best of first-place finishers in seven categories.

Cetrella Bistro and Café

845 Main Street
Half Moon Bay, California 94019
650-726-4090
www.cetrella.com

Prince Edward Island Mussels Steamed with Pastis and Tomato

By Chef Lewis Rossman

Serves 4

INGREDIENTS

2 lbs Prince Edward Island mussels
2 Tbs olive oil
1/2 cup white onion, diced
1 Tbs chopped garlic
1 Tbs chopped anchovy
1 tsp harissa

3 oz pastis
1 cup white wine
4 oz tomato sauce
2 Tbs butter
2 Tbs chopped chervil
Salt and pepper, to taste

PREPARATION INSTRUCTIONS

Place mussels, olive oil, onion, garlic, anchovies and harissa in a shallow pot on medium heat. When the mussels start to open add the pastis. Allow to burn off, then add the white wine and tomato sauce. Cover and allow to steam for 3-5 minutes until all mussels have opened. Finish with the butter and chervil. Season with salt and pepper.

ABOUT THE CHEF

Chef Lewis Rossman was raised in Philadelphia, the oldest of five children. He grew up in a very healthy environment with a mother of Italian heritage and father of Russian heritage. Rossman went to college at Syracuse University where he first found a niche in cooking. Shortly after college he moved to San Francisco to pursue a career as a chef. He studied at the California Culinary Academy in the city and worked at the well known restaurants Acquerello and Kokkari before helping open Cetrella almost five years ago. Rossman became the Executive Chef two years ago, and the restaurant has reached further acclaim under his guidance. He has traveled throughout the Mediterranean and other parts of the world.

SUGGESTED WINE PAIRING

- 2004 Cantina Terlano Pinot Bianco, Alto Adige

THE STORY BEHIND THE RECIPE

This is a recipe that was developed for Cetrella. It is dear to me because as a child we would frequent a small Italian restaurant in South Philadelphia and always share buckets of mussels marinara. This is a simple recipe that works well for the home cook. It is an item that people come to Cetrella expecting to see on the menu. This is saying quite a bit because we change our menu every day.

Cézanne

1740 Ocean Avenue
Santa Monica, California 90401
310-395-9700
www.lemerigothotel.com

CÉZANNE

Short Ribs with Gnocchi, Wild Mushrooms and Foie Gras

By Chef Desi Szonntagh

Serves 4

INGREDIENTS

Short Ribs:
12 oz short ribs (3 pieces per serving)
3 qts chicken stock
4 carrots
2 stalks celery
4 leeks, split and cleaned
1 head garlic, split
3 sprigs thyme
Salt and pepper, to taste

Gnocchi:
3 baked potatoes
4 egg yolks
1 cup semolina flour
1/2 cup Parmesan, grated
2 Tbs butter

Red Wine Sauce:
3 cups cabernet
Pinch thyme
2 shallots, sliced
2 cloves garlic
2 cups demi glaze

Wild Mushrooms and Foie Gras:
10 oz mixed wild mushrooms
   (chanterelles, shiitake, porcini)
2 shallots, minced
2 cloves garlic, chopped
Salt and pepper, to taste
4 Tbs butter
2-1/2 oz foie gras (4 pieces)
8 asparagus spears, blanched
8 baby carrots, blanched

PREPARATION INSTRUCTIONS

Short Ribs: Place the short ribs into a heavy stock pot with chicken stock, carrots, celery, leeks, garlic, thyme, salt and pepper and bring to a boil. Turn down and simmer for about 1-1/2 hours, until the meat is falling away from the bone. Remove the ribs, keeping them intact, and place onto a platter to cool. Discard vegetables and reserve stock to use in reheating the short ribs.

Gnocchi: Bake potatoes about 45 minutes, till soft. Cook egg yolks in a mixing bowl over simmering water like sabayon. Scoop the cooked potatoes out of their skins and immediately push through a ricer. Combine flour and parmesan with the yolks and potatoes. Bring 1 quart of water to boil and, making quenelle shapes with a teaspoon, poach in the water until they rise to the top. Reserve 16 pieces. The rest can be saved for other dishes or frozen.

Red Wine Sauce: Reduce the cabernet with thyme, shallots and garlic until syrupy. Add demi glaze and bring to a boil. Reserve and keep hot.

Wild Mushrooms and Foie Gras: Sauté the wild mushrooms with shallots, garlic and half of the butter until tender. Reserve and keep warm. To serve, cut the short ribs off the bone into 1-inch squares and warm up in the chicken stock. Sauté the four pieces of foie gras on both sides until medium rare and remove from the pan, keeping warm. Heat up remaining butter and sauté the blanched asparagus and carrots. Toss the gnocchi in butter to heat up.

Plating: Align four plates and spoon the mushrooms in the middle of each. Top with foie gras. Arrange around the plate the short rib squares (3 per order), asparagus, carrots and gnocchi. Drizzle with red wine sauce and serve.

ABOUT THE CHEF

Chef Desi Szonntagh continues to create culinary "art" as the Executive Chef of Cézanne Restaurant at Le Merigot Beach Hotel and Spa in the vibrant beach city of Santa Monica, California. This seasoned chef is taking the restaurant in a new direction by firing up Provençal cuisine and further raising the restaurant's profile. Prior to joining Le Merigot, Szonntagh was the Executive Sous Chef at the acclaimed Terrace Restaurant at Hotel Bel Air in Bel Air, CA, where he created a menu that earned the restaurant accolades in the pages of *Saveur* magazine. Szonntagh is delighted to lead the Cézanne team, where he continues to fascinate diners with his culinary surprises. Szonntagh has more than 20 years of experience working as a chef for an impressive roster of fine dining establishments, including Shutters on the Beach in Santa Monica, CA; 2087, an American bistro in Thousand Oaks, CA, where he was partner/chef and received an exemplary review from the *Los Angeles Times* restaurant critic Irene Virbilla; Tatou in Tokyo, Beverly Hills, Aspen and New York City; Provence Restaurant, New York City; LaBoheme, New York City and Le Cirque, New York City. In addition to his extensive experience in these renowned restaurants, Szonntagh was named as a featured chef at the James Beard House.

SUGGESTED WINE PAIRING

- A light red wine such as a Pinot Noir like 2004 Wild Horse or 2003 Acacia
- A darker red, such as a 2001 Jordon Cabernet Sauvignon

Chan Dara
Larchmont

310 North Larchmont Boulevard
Los Angeles, California 90004
323-467-1052
www.chandarawestla.com

Seafood Pad Thai

By Chef Buzz Fukutomi

Serves 1

INGREDIENTS

Noodles:
1 lb wet small rice noodles
1 Tbs oil

Stir-Fry:
2 Tbs oil
1 Tbs minced garlic
1 Tbs chili
1/4 lb shelled shrimp, deveined and rinsed
2 eggs
1-1/2 Tbs fish sauce
1-1/2 Tbs tamarind sauce
1 Tbs sugar

1/4 tsp paprika powder
1/3 lb bean sprouts
1 Tbs crushed peanuts
1/2 lb steamed rock clams
1/2 lb steamed black mussels

Garnish:
1/4 lb steamed king crabmeat
Crushed peanuts
Lime wedge

PREPARATION INSTRUCTIONS

Devein shrimp, rinse and drain.

Noodles: Heat 1 tablespoon oil and stir-fry noodles until hot.

Stir-fry: In separate pan, heat 2 tablespoons oil, then stir-fry garlic and chili until fragrant. Add shrimp, stir-fry until color changes. Add eggs and stir-fry until slightly dry. Add fish sauce, tamarind sauce, sugar, paprika powder, bean sprouts and crushed peanut, and stir-fry briefly. Add clams and mussels and stir-fry. Combine with noodles.

Plating: Put on a plate and top with crabmeat. Sprinkle more crushed peanut on top, and serve with lime wedge, if desired.

HELPFUL HINTS, VARIATIONS OR OTHER ADVICE

1/2 lb dry small rice noodles soaked and softened in cold water will double in weight to 1 lb. Add water if too dry during stir-frying.

ABOUT THE CHEF

Buzz Fukutomi earned his degree at the Southern California School of Culinary Arts (1998).
Buzz is a California, National and International Food Handler.

SUGGESTED WINE PAIRING

• 2001 Talbott Chardonnay

THE STORY BEHIND THE RECIPE

Pad Thai is the most popular food in Thailand. It's also known as a national Thai dish. I created this recipe in order to represent Thailand, a beautiful country. This is my personal favorite.

Chez Melange

1716 South Pacific Coast Highway
Redondo Beach, California 90277
310-316-1566
www.chezmelange.com

Clam and Corn Fritters

By Chef Robert Bell

Serves 4

INGREDIENTS

3 cups flour
2 tsp baking powder
2 eggs
2 Tbs olive oil
2 tsp salt
1-1/2 cups mixed cheese (cheddar, jack, mozzarella)

2-1/2 cups fresh corn (blanched for 2 minutes)
1-1/2 cups fresh creamed corn
1/4 cup chopped garlic
1/2 bunch cilantro, chopped
2-3 jalapenos, chopped
1-1/2 cups clams (canned with juice drained)

PREPARATION INSTRUCTIONS

Combine all ingredients well. Form into 1"-2" balls. Fry at 350°F in deep fat with vegetable oil until golden brown (3 to 5 minutes).

Garnish:
Serve with a mango fruit salsa.

HELPFUL HINTS, VARIATIONS OR OTHER ADVICE

Simple, easy and good when entertaining. Perfect as a beginning course.

ABOUT THE CHEF

Robert Bell's passion for food began as a young boy in New York City growing up at the heels of his Italian grandmother. Every Sunday Grandma would have the whole family over for supper. Those days were full of family, conversation, work and delectable meals. In his teens, Robert's family moved to Hollywood, CA. While at Los Angeles Community College he worked part time in several restaurants. Starting as a dishwasher, then busser, then a server, Robert ended up in the kitchen where he finally found an outlet for his passion and talent. Working his way up through the trenches was how Robert learned the culinary profession. Back then culinary school was not a real option. After graduating college, Robert worked in the architecture field for over 15 years. It was there that he met Chuck Lehman, a gentleman who was opening a restaurant in Hermosa Beach. Realizing that something had been missing in his life, Robert quit the architecture firm and started working with Chuck at the Hermosa restaurant, Courtney's.

It was at Courtney Foods that Robert met Michael Franks. In 1982 the partners opened Chez Melange, a popular, upscale restaurant in Redondo Beach. Christine's and Misto Caffe and Bakery, both in Hillside Village in Torrance, followed in 1989 and 1990. Michael and Robert's fourth restaurant, Depot, opened in the fall of 1991 in downtown Torrance. They also opened a new fast food concept in Rolling Hills Plaza, Annie's Pantry, as well as Chez Allez, a gourmet shop and café, in December of 1998.

In 1999 Michael and Robert were appointed as consultants and managers for the food service at the Ocean Trails Golf Course. Chez Melange was voted #1 eclectic restaurant in Los Angeles and South Bay's #1 restaurant in the 2001 *Los Angeles Guide*, as well as placing fourth for the *Los Angeles Times'* Best Wine List, and was designated a Gold Star Restaurant and a Four Star Restaurant by the Southern California Restaurant Writers. The Epicurean Rendezvous named Chez Melange one of the top 100 Restaurants in Los Angeles, and *Restaurant Hospitality* named it as one of the country's top 500 restaurants. In 1990, Robert received the prestigious award of "Restaurateur of the Year" by both the California Restaurant Writers Association and the Southern California Restaurant Writers Association.

In 1991, Robert was named "Citizen of the Year" by the Wellness Community of the South Bay. For the last 15 years Wine Spectator has given Chez Melange their award for one of the best wine lists in the United States. In 1988 Robert founded a culinary scholarship program for local high school students, "Young Chefs of South Bay," a program designed to introduce young people to the restaurant industry at an early age. The "Young Chef's Program" has since taken off, and now reaches a broad range of Southern California High Schools.

SUGGESTED WINE PAIRING

• 2004 Rombauer Chardonnay, Napa Valley

THE STORY BEHIND THE RECIPE

This is comfort food, although the fruit salsa adds a lightness and freshness to the dish.

Croce's Restaurant & Jazz Bar

802 Fifth Avenue
San Diego, California 92101
619-233-4355
www.croces.com

Croce's Grilled Swordfish with Mediterranean Green Olive Tapenade

By Chef Ingrid Croce and Chef James Clark

Serves 6

INGREDIENTS

Tapenade:
1 red bell pepper
1/4 cup green olives, sliced
1/4 cup canned artichoke hearts, diced
1 Tbs capers
1 Tbs sun-dried tomatoes, sliced
Juice of 3 lemons
2 Tbs fresh parsley, chopped
2 tsp garlic, minced
1/4 cup olive oil

Coulis:
2 red bell peppers
1/2 teaspoon garlic, minced
1 Tbs olive oil
1/4 cup sherry wine
2 Tbs fresh basil, chopped
6 Tbs vegetable broth
2 Tbs half-and-half
Salt and pepper, to taste

Orzo:
1 lb orzo
1/4 cup olive oil
5 cups vegetable broth
5 garlic cloves, roasted
1 Tbs olive oil

1 Tbs honey
1 Tbs fresh oregano, chopped

Swordfish:
2-1/2 lbs fresh center-cut swordfish
2 Tbs olive oil
Salt and pepper, to taste
2 lemons
2 Tbs Parmesan cheese, grated
1-1/2 lbs baby spinach
Salt and pepper, to taste

Garnish:
Lemon slices
6 sprigs fresh parsley

PREPARATION INSTRUCTIONS

Tapenade:
Roast 1 red pepper on a grill or in a 400º oven until darkened on all sides. Place in a plastic bag to cool. Carefully peel off outer skin. Remove seeds and dice. In a mixing bowl, combine roasted red pepper, olives, artichoke hearts, capers, sun-dried tomatoes, lemon juice, parsley, garlic and olive oil. Refrigerate. Can be made a day in advance.

(cont'd)

ABOUT THE CHEF

Executive Chef Ingrid Croce, celebrity, author and owner of the esteemed Croce's Restaurant & Jazz Bar in downtown San Diego's historic Gaslamp District, has been a visionary in San Diego's dining scene for over 20 years. Croce is credited with helping to bring about San Diego's culinary revolution. Named by The San Diego Business Journal as one of the top ten businesswomen in the city, Croce has also been honored by the California Restaurant Association as Restaurateur of the Year. Her books include *Thyme in a Bottle*, an autobiographical cookbook, and the brand new *San Diego Restaurant* Cookbook, which features more than 260 signature recipes from San Diego's most treasured eateries and personal biographies of over 130 restaurateurs, hoteliers, chefs and vendors.

PREPARATION INSTRUCTIONS *(cont'd)*

Coulis:

Roast 2 red bell peppers as above, seed and dice. In a small pan, sweat 1/2 teaspoon minced garlic in 1 tablespoon olive oil and deglaze the pan with sherry. Add peppers, basil and 6 tablespoons of the vegetable broth. Simmer for 10 minutes. Purée in a blender with half-and-half. Season with salt and pepper. Can be made 1 day in advance.

Orzo:

In a heavy sauté pan, cook orzo in 1/4 cup olive oil until golden brown. Deglaze with the rest of the vegetable broth. Bring to a boil. Cook until pasta is al dente. Strain and cool. In a separate sauté pan, cook whole garlic cloves in 1 tablespoon olive oil over low-to-medium heat until golden brown. Remove from heat and toss in honey. Toss orzo with roasted garlic and oregano. Should be prepared as close to service as possible.

Swordfish:

Cut swordfish into 6 equal steaks. Coat with 1 tablespoon olive oil and season with salt and pepper. Place on hot grill and squeeze 1 lemon over all steaks. Cook for 5-7 minutes. Turn over. Squeeze 1 lemon over all steaks again. Place 1/4 cup tapenade on each steak. Sprinkle with Parmesan cheese. In a sauté pan, heat 1 Tbs olive oil and toss spinach until wilted. Season with salt and pepper.

Plating:

Arrange spinach in a ring in the center of a serving plate, leaving enough room for orzo to be placed in the middle. Place cooked swordfish on top of orzo and drizzle red pepper coulis around spinach. Garnish with lemon slices and sprigs of parsley.

The Cupcake Corner

29911 Muledeer Lane
Castaic, California 91384
661-618-3628
www.thecupcakecorner.net

....

Chocolate Macadamia Nut Bread Pudding with Warm Vanilla Caramel Sauce

By Chef Cindy Schwanke

Serves 10

INGREDIENTS

15 (3-oz) butter croissants
15 egg yolks
10 oz granulated sugar
1 vanilla bean
6-1/2 cups + 1 Tbs heavy cream
1 lb toasted macadamia nuts
1-1/2 lbs bittersweet chocolate

Vanilla Caramel Sauce:
1 lb granulated sugar
1/3 cup water
1/2 tsp lemon juice
2 Tbs corn syrup
1-1/2 cups heavy cream
2 oz butter

PREPARATION INSTRUCTIONS

Generously butter a 9" x 13" pan or 12 4-oz ramekins. Cut the croissants into bite-sized pieces. Spread croissant pieces into the prepared pan. In separate bowl, mix yolks and sugar. Add vanilla bean and heavy cream. Pour this mixture over the croissants. Add toasted macadamia nuts and chocolate to the pan. Bake at 350°F for about 40 minutes.

Vanilla Caramel Sauce:

Boil sugar, water and lemon juice. Add corn syrup. Let turn amber color. Add cream and butter. Remove from heat and let sit for about 20 minutes. Pour over bread pudding mixture. Enjoy!

HELPFUL HINTS, VARIATIONS OR OTHER ADVICE

The base mixture can be used to make a variety of bread puddings.

ABOUT THE CHEF

Cindy Schwanke has her Associate's Degree in the Culinary Arts. She has worked in bake shops for over 15 years and has been a pastry chef for about 3 years. She has participated in many competitions and also teaches pastry classes to adults and children. She interned at Spago restaurant with Sherry Yard. She has worked in all elements of the pastry industry including restaurants, hotels and catering. She is currently opening a bake shop of her own, The Cupcake Corner.

SUGGESTED WINE PAIRING

• Any quality Port

THE STORY BEHIND THE RECIPE

I used to make this recipe for the Sunday brunch crowd at the Hyatt hotel in Valencia. I would always get great compliments on this certain dessert. One Sunday a special client requested this dessert and was very happy when I made it for him and his family. The next day I received two dozen roses from the client thanking me for the awesome dessert. I will never forget that moment.

Devonian International

8283 Grove Avenue, Suite 203
Rancho Cucamonga, California 91730
909-949-8979

....

Rosemary Chicken

By Chef Elliot Weinstein

Serves 4

INGREDIENTS

2 lbs boneless chicken breast
1 large brown onion, sliced thin
16-20 sprigs fresh rosemary

Granulated garlic
Salt and pepper
2 Tbs olive oil

PREPARATION INSTRUCTIONS

Place half the sliced onions on bottom of pan. Lay half the rosemary sprigs on the onions. Lightly season the chicken breasts with the salt, pepper and granulated garlic. Put the chicken breasts on the rosemary. Cover the chicken breasts with the remaining sliced onions and rosemary sprigs. Drizzle the oil on the chicken. Place in the oven at 350°F. The breasts will cook in about 35 minutes (turn over about half way through).

HELPFUL HINTS, VARIATIONS OR OTHER ADVICE

Cut chicken can be used for a more rustic dish. Serve with roasted potatoes, garnish with rosemary. Other fresh herbs such as bay leaf, oregano and lavender can be used with the rosemary for variation.

SUGGESTED WINE PAIRING

- Chardonnay, or any dry white

THE STORY BEHIND THE RECIPE

This recipe is a favorite with our catering company and many happy customers. Even though it is simple, it is very tasty. We have used this recipe, a personal favorite, for many years.

Dinner du Jour Catering

Redondo Beach, California 90278

310-372-9457

www.dinnerdujour.net

Zesty Lemon Bars

By Chef Bette Fraser

Yields 30

INGREDIENTS

Crust:
3 cups flour
3/4 cup powdered sugar
1 cup butter

Filling:
4 eggs
2 cups sugar
1/3 cup fresh lemon juice

1 tsp lemon extract
1/4 cup flour
1/2 tsp baking powder
Lemon zest

PREPARATION INSTRUCTIONS

Crust:

In a food processor, mix flour with powdered sugar. Cut in the butter until fine crumbs form. Line a 1/2 sheet pan with parchment paper. Press mixture into pan. Bake at 325°F for 20 minutes or until golden.

Filling:

Meanwhile, in a medium mixing bowl, beat eggs until foamy. Gradually add sugar, lemon juice and extract until fluffy. Sift flour and baking powder over mixture and combine gently. Pour onto crust and top with grated lemon zest. Return to the oven for 20-25 minutes. When cool, sift powdered sugar on top and cut into squares. Enjoy!

ABOUT THE CHEF

Dinner du Jour Catering is located in Redondo Beach, CA and has been serving the South Bay and Southern California area since 1991. Prior to opening Dinner du Jour, chef/owner Bette Fraser made candy under the label Bette's Brittle, as featured in *Food & Wine* Magazine. Chef Bette attended Le Cordon Bleu and the Ritz Escoffier Ecole de Gastronomie Francaise in Paris, France. In 2004 and 2005, Bette attended "Cucina e Vino," cooking with Giuliano Hazan in Verona, Italy. She is a graduate of the University of Southern California.

THE STORY BEHIND THE RECIPE

This heavenly bar cookie recipe has been in our family for years. It has been one of the most popular and often-requested dessert items that I serve while catering parties.

El Pollo Loco

3333 Michelson Drive, Suite 550
Irvine, California
949-399-2072
www.elpolloloco.com

Chicken Tortilla Soup

By Chef Jonathan Rogan

Serves 8

INGREDIENTS

2 qts prepared chicken broth
1 whole El Pollo Loco Chicken
1 fresh poblano pepper, roasted and diced
1 cup fresh carrots, diced 1/4-inch thick
1 cup fresh celery, diced 1/4-inch thick
1 ear fresh corn
1 cup pico de gallo (salsa) from El Pollo Loco
1 tsp cumin, ground
1 tsp dried Mexican oregano, crushed or to taste
1/2 tsp ground coriander seed

1/4 tsp garlic powder
1 fresh lime, juiced
Salt and pepper to taste

Garnish:
1 oz Queso Cotija, finely crumbled
1 bunch fresh cilantro, chopped, stems discarded
8 corn tortillas, cut into 1/4-inch strips
2 cups corn oil (for tortilla frying)

PREPARATION INSTRUCTIONS

Shred meat off the bones of a whole El Pollo Loco chicken. Discard bones and skin. Cool if necessary. Roast poblano pepper over an open flame on your stove or in a hot pan until the skin is charred and blistered evenly. Place in a paper bag to steam and then cool. While the pepper is cooling, wash and dice vegetables (carrots, celery, cilantro) and set aside. Cut the corn off the cob and set aside. Destem and seed the roasted poblano pepper and scrape off the skin with a knife. Dice into 1/4-inch pieces and set aside. Crumble the Queso Cotija and set aside. Heat oil to approximately 350°F. Fry the tortilla strips in corn oil in a 6" deep sauce pot or deep fryer. Use enough oil to slightly submerge strips. Cook for about 60 seconds or until crispy, but don't let them get too dark. Remove from oil and allow to drain well on paper towels set into a bowl. Set aside.

In a medium saucepot combine the broth, all vegetables (except cilantro), and 8 oz El Pollo Loco's pico de gallo and seasonings. Bring to a boil over high heat. Lower heat to simmer and add shredded chicken; allow to simmer another 20 minutes. Immediately prior to serving, squeeze in fresh lime and stir. Portion into warm bowls and garnish each with a healthy dose of tortilla strips, fresh chopped cilantro and Queso Cotija, if desired. Enjoy!

HELPFUL HINTS, VARIATIONS OR OTHER ADVICE

Try adding slices of fresh California Haas Avocado or increase the spice with some roasted habanero chile.

ABOUT THE CHEF

Jonathan Rogan is the Manager of Culinary Development for El Pollo Loco. Chef Rogan translates his culinary vision into menu creation and recipe development in the El Pollo Loco test kitchen. His passion for quality and freshness infuses his approach to product formulation and testing. Chef Rogan's impressive culinary journey began when he graduated with honors from the highly regarded Western Culinary Institute in Portland, Oregon. He furthered his pursuit of gourmet greatness by continuing at The Culinary Institute of America-Greystone Campus in Napa Valley and at Johnson & Wales University in Providence, Rhode Island, successfully completing numerous advanced culinary programs. Prior to joining El Pollo Loco, Chef Rogan honed his culinary skills for over twenty years at many food and beverage businesses, including Good Earth Restaurants, California Pizza Kitchen, Gelson's Markets, Square One Restaurant and Moose McGillycuddy's Pub & Café. Chef Rogan also has more than ten years of product development experience in senior culinary positions with Huxtables' Kitchens, Sizzler USA, Webvan Group, Chi-Chi's Mexican Restaurants and Perspectives/The Consulting Group. Chef Rogan is a member of the Research Chef's Association, Institute of Food Technologists (Foodservice Division) and Restaurant Business Magazine (Advisory Board). He is also NRA ServSafe® Certified.

SUGGESTED WINE PAIRING

- 2002 Zind-Humbrecht Gewurztraminer Herrenweg de Turckheim, Alsace
- Your favorite 100% Agave Blanco Tequila
- A cold Modelo Negro

THE STORY BEHIND THE RECIPE

This recipe is adapted from the popular Chicken Tortilla Soup we serve in El Pollo Loco restaurants. The soup features our delicious citrus-marinated, flame-grilled chicken and has quickly become a favorite on our menu. It provides bold flavor.

Fabiolus Café

6270 Sunset Boulevard
Hollywood, California 90028
323-467-2882
www.fabiolus.net

Bigoli All`Anatra

By Chef Maria Chiara Santi

Serves 8

INGREDIENTS

4 duck legs (with or without skin)
1 large onion
2 celery stalks
1 large carrot
6 Tbs extra virgin olive oil
Salt and pepper, as needed
1-1/4 cups red wine (Valpolicella is recommended)
2 cups tomatoes, peeled
1 sprig rosemary
2 bay leaves

Pasta:
24 oz dry semolina durum pasta—use thick spaghetti,
    or any other pasta of your choice ("Bigoli" is homemade
    thick, rustic spaghetti originally from Verona, Italy)
1-1/2 gal water
1 Tbs salt

PREPARATION INSTRUCTIONS

Finely chop onion, celery and carrot. In a large pot heat extra virgin olive oil and add chopped vegetables. Lower the heat if necessary and gently tenderize the mixture. Once soft, add duck legs, season with salt and ground black pepper. Roast the duck in the "soffritto," and once roasted, add red wine, peeled tomatoes (blended or chopped with their juice), bay leaves and rosemary sprig (tied together). Lower heat, cover pan and let simmer for about 1-1/2 to 2 hours. Liquid should be reduced to a sauce consistency. Cook a little more if the sauce is too watery.

Remove legs and tied rosemary and bay leaves from sauce and let cool. Once at room temperature, remove duck meat from bones and discard skin (if present). Cut meat into small pieces. If you prefer a smooth texture you can blend the sauce, otherwise recombine meat with sauce.

Pasta:
Boil a large pot of water (1-1/2 gal). Once boiling add one tablespoon salt and pasta. Cook pasta al dente
(8-9 minutes), drain. On a large serving plate combine pasta, sprinkle with grated Parmesan cheese, mix and add sauce. Stir and serve. Buon Appetito!

HELPFUL HINTS, VARIATIONS OR OTHER ADVICE

Any pasta will go well with this sauce. The bigoli are the best, because the surface is very rough and holds the sauce well. We prepare this and other homemade pasta at Fabiolus Café.

ABOUT THE CHEF

Maria Chiara Santi has owned and run a restaurant-pizzeria on the beautiful hills surrounding the Garda Lake on the Verona side for 13 years. Maria moved to California five years ago and married her big love Fabio three years ago. She is now developing recipes, specials and special events for their two restaurants. She also handles the fresh pasta preparation.

SUGGESTED WINE PAIRING

• 2003 Santi Valpolicella Ripasso, "Solane"

THE STORY BEHIND THE RECIPE

This dish in the classic recipe does not use meat, only the sauce and the juice obtained from it. We changed it around a little bit, because here in the United States people like really thick and consistent sauce. With the meat addition the sauce result is less fatty than the original one. Our customers love this dish and it has been published in the *Los Angeles Times* in the food section. If you do not use Bigoli, you can change the name to a more general, "Pasta all`Anatra."

Five Crowns Restaurant

3801 East Coast Highway
Corona Del Mar, California 92625
949-760-0555
www.lawrysonline.com

Potato-Crusted Roast Salmon with a Three-Mustard Sauce

By Chef Dennis Brask

Serves 4

INGREDIENTS

Salmon:
4 salmon filets (1" thick, approximately 8 oz each)
3 potatoes, cooked and shredded
2 Tbs horseradish root, freshly grated
3 Tbs butter, clarified
Salt and white pepper, to taste

Three Mustard Sauce:
2 tsp shallots, chopped
1 tsp butter

1 cup fish stock or clam juice
2 Tbs Dijon mustard
1 Tbs dry mustard
1-1/2 Tbs whole grain mustard
2 Tbs cornstarch
2 cups white wine
1/4 cup heavy cream
Salt and white pepper, to taste

PREPARATION INSTRUCTIONS

Salmon:
Season salmon filets with salt and white pepper and arrange on a nonstick baking sheet. In a stainless steel bowl combine potatoes, horseradish, butter and seasoning, tossing gently to combine. Portion potato mixture on top of salmon filets and lightly press down. Bake in the upper third of a preheated 425°F oven for 18-20 minutes, or until potato topping is brown and crusty.

Three-Mustard Sauce:
In a small saucepan sauté shallots in butter until transparent. Add fish stock and the three mustards, bring to a boil, thicken with cornstarch and add white wine. Add cream and return to a simmer. Cook gently for five minutes and adjust seasonings. Pool sauce on four plates and top with the roasted salmon.

HELPFUL HINTS, VARIATIONS OR OTHER ADVICE

The potatoes called for in this recipe are peeled baked Russets. Utilizing some of the market's unusual varieties such as Yukon Gold or Peruvian Purple potatoes can add a new dimension to the presentation. If you can, obtain smoked fish bones for the stock.

ABOUT THE CHEF

Born in Minnesota, Dennis Brask grew up in Hopkins, a suburb of the Twin Cities. Dennis studied engineering at Normandale Junior College and the University of Minnesota, working his way through by cooking in the kitchens of a hospital and the North Star Inn, downtown. It was here that his life as a culinarian began. Brask spent all of his early years in the hotel environment working his way around the kitchen under a variety of German, Austrian and other European chefs in both Minnesota and Milwaukee, Wisconsin. Dennis's career as Executive Chef began at the Marc Plaza Hotel and carried on through Playboy Hotels and Intercontinental Hotels in Wisconsin and Florida. In 1983 Dennis was hired as Executive Chef at the Five Crowns Restaurant. He was instrumental in revamping and implementing regular menu cycles. Dennis left Five Crowns in 1990 and was Opening General Manager for the Summit House in Fullerton. He returned to Five Crowns as Executive Chef in 1995.

Dennis is very active in charity events. He is an avid supporter of Share Ourselves and the Orange County Interfaith Shelter. He has represented the Five Crowns at the Taste of Newport and the Christmas Company, a major fund raiser for the Junior League of Orange County, as well as his newly adopted cause, the American Liver Foundation, in memory of his brother David. Dennis Brask resides in Laguna Beach with his wife, Margo.

SUGGESTED WINE PAIRING

- Sauvignon Blanc
- Chardonnay
- Pinot Noir

THE STORY BEHIND THE RECIPE

This dish became a signature item for the restaurant back in the 1990's, by popular demand. I first ran it as a daily special, and it outsold any other fish preparation by a large margin. Fueled by this success, I moved it up to a seasonal offering where it continued to move better than any other presentation we had offered. I continued to menu this dish until I was encouraged to offer a different dish on the menu to ensure variety in our offerings. The restaurant's guests were outraged and started a letter-writing campaign to the corporate office to "bring our salmon back." Since then we have not dared to tamper with this recipe.

Ford's Filling Station

9531 Culver Boulevard
Culver City, California 90232
310-280-0861
www.fordsfillingstation.net

Crispy Flattened Chicken

By Chef Ben Ford

Serves 8

INGREDIENTS

4 halved whole chickens (boned)
1/4 cup olive oil

Chicken Spices:
1 bay leaf
2 whole cloves
2 Tbs coriander seeds
2 Tbs cumin seeds
2 Tbs fennel seeds

Lemon Garlic Confit:
1/2 cup olive oil
9 to 12 garlic cloves
1 bay leaf
Zest of 1/2 lemon

Succotash:
1/2 Tbs olive oil
3 Tbs fennel bulb, diced
Lemon garlic confit
1 cup black-eyed peas
2 cups cut yellow corn (kernels)
Salt and pepper, to taste
1/2 cup chicken stock
3 Tbs butter
1 cup leaf spinach

PREPARATION INSTRUCTIONS

Chicken Spices:

In a sauté pan, toast all ingredients to a golden brown. Let cool and grind. Set aside for chicken.

Chicken:

Take halved chickens and salt, skin side first, turn over and add chicken spice lightly, with salt. Heat pan with olive oil (roughly 1/4 cup). Start with skin side down and cook lightly to a golden brown color. Turn over and cook bone side down to a golden brown color. Heat oven to 400°F and finish cooking (approximately 15-20 minutes).

Lemon Garlic Confit:

Cook olive oil, garlic cloves and bay leaf on medium heat until cloves are al dente. Remove from heat and add lemon zest. Let cool to room temperature and set aside for succotash.

Succotash:

Heat olive oil. Add fennel and sear. Add lemon garlic confit, black-eyed peas, corn kernels and salt and pepper to taste. Add chicken stock and reduce by half. Add butter at the end to thicken. Toss in spinach.

Plating:

Plate with mash (optional) and succotash on opposite sides of plate. Lay chicken atop succotash.

ABOUT THE CHEF

Ben Ford is one of California's brightest culinary stars, having earned his kitchen stripes at such distinguished institutions as The Farm of Beverly Hills, Opus and Campanile. Ford's epicurean journey began at the University of Dijon in the heart of Burgundy, France, where he was inspired by Europe's Slow Food movement. After completing formal training at the California Culinary Academy in San Francisco, Ford further sharpened his talents with one of the country's finest organic chefs, Alice Waters of Chez Panisse. In 1999 Ford opened Chadwick, marrying his rich professional experience with a personal commitment to organic and artisanal sensibilities. As always, Ford drew inspiration from his mother, Mary Ford, a fine cook and illustrator, and from his father, actor Harrison Ford, a skilled craftsman and artist of great integrity. With Ford's Filling Station, Ford turns the traditional British gastropub concept into something decidedly American. Letting individual ingredients shine through is a hallmark of Ford's philosophy, and an approach that has won high praise from critics and diners. A father of one, Ford donates much of his time to charitable food events, and is a Chef Chair for Taste of the Nation, benefiting the Share Our Strength organization.

SUGGESTED WINE PAIRING

• 2000 Rottlan Torra Priorat Reserva, Catalonia

The French Gourmet

960 Turquoise Street
San Diego, California 92109
858-488-1725
www.thefrenchgourmet.com

THE FRENCH GOURMET

Avocado Salad Delight

By Chef Michel Malécot

Serves 4

INGREDIENTS

Dressing:
1-1/2 tsp ginger root
1 clove garlic
1 shallot
1/4 cup red wine vinegar
3/4 cup low sodium soy sauce
1 Tbs sweet chili sauce
2 Tbs honey
1/2 tsp chili, crushed

4 Tbs sesame oil
4 Tbs olive oil
1/4 bunch cilantro

Salad:
2 whole avocados, cut
6 cherry tomatoes
1 grapefruit, segmented
4 cups mixed greens, cleaned and cut

PREPARATION INSTRUCTIONS

Dressing:

Blend dressing ingredients together. Cover and refrigerate while preparing the salad.

Avocado Salad:

Cut avocados and save skins/shells as bowls for serving salad. Cut cherry tomatoes in half. Segment grapefruit. Mix cut-up avocado with halved cherry tomatoes and segmented grapefruit. Put mixed salad greens in the 4 avocado shells.

Plating:

Serve avocado mixture over greens in shells, garnish with a slice of grapefruit on top. Spoon 1-1/2 tablespoons of dressing over each salad.

ABOUT THE CHEF

Michel Malécot, founder and President of The French Gourmet, is known throughout San Diego for his expertise as a caterer and for the quality of his menus and food. Michel is the recipient of many prestigious awards from the hospitality industry, various associations and even the government of France. He has been awarded the very prestigious Gold Key Award for Food & Beverage Person of the Year by the California Restaurant Association, San Diego Chapter, has been voted top caterer by several local publications and, most recently, won the Torch Award for Marketplace Ethics presented by the Better Business Bureau. The French Gourmet has served San Diego's social, corporate and wedding markets with what many consider the city's finest full-service catering since 1979, offering high-quality menu suggestions ranging from office luncheons to elaborate dinner events. Clients include many Fortune 500 and publicly owned companies. Besides professional event planning, the company has all the resources required for a successful event, from floral décor to alcoholic beverage service to equipment rental.

Frenchy's Bistro

4137 East Anaheim Street
Long Beach, California 90804
562-494-8787
www.frenchysbistro.com

....

Tuna Burgers

By Chef Andre Angles

Serves 4

INGREDIENTS

Tuna Burgers:
2 lbs fresh chilled tuna
4 cloves garlic, minced
1/4 cup extra virgin olive oil
4 anchovies, minced
1/4 cup basil, minced
Salt and ground pepper
Extra virgin olive oil
Red wine vinegar

Assembly:
4 hamburger buns
1 large tomato, thinly sliced
4 lettuce leaves

PREPARATION INSTRUCTIONS

Thinly slice tuna; chop and mix with garlic, olive oil, anchovies, basil, salt and pepper. Divide mixture into 4 balls for 1" thick patties. Refrigerate 30 minutes before cooking. Immediately before cooking burgers, douse buns with olive oil and vinegar. Sear tuna burgers one minute on each side. Line with tomato and lettuce. Place over buns and serve immediately.

HELPFUL HINTS, VARIATIONS OR OTHER ADVICE

Instead of olive oil and vinegar try spreading sesame mayonnaise on the buns. This recipe can be also made in small bite-size burgers as hors d'oeuvres for receptions.

ABOUT THE CHEF

Born in Avignon, France, Chef Andre Angles went to culinary school for three years and pastry school for one year. He's worked in France, Holland, Switzerland and the U.S. He has also worked with legendary chef Roger Verge at Le Moulin de Mougins, at L'Orangerie Los Angeles, L'Hermitage and La Grotte. He then opened Frenchy's Bistro in Long Beach in 1996 and has been highly rated 27/30 by Zagat since opening.

SUGGESTED WINE PAIRING

- 2002 Trimbach Pinot Blanc
- 2003 Domaine Mellot Sancerre, Alsace
- 2004 Chateau Souverain Sauvignon Blanc, Loire
- 2004 Clos Pepe Estate Chardonnay "Homage to Chablis" Santa Rita Hills

THE STORY BEHIND THE RECIPE

I learned this recipe while working briefly with Michel Richard at Citrus; it has been one of my all-time favorites for its originality and taste.

Fresco Café

3987 State Street, Suite B
Santa Barbara, California 93105
805-967-6037
www.frescosb.com
www.santabarbarainn.com/dining

Fresh Lime Coconut Cake with Lime Zest Buttercream

By Chef Mark Brouillard

Serves 12

INGREDIENTS

Cake:
3 cups cake flour
2 cups granulated sugar
2-1/2 tsp baking powder
1/2 tsp salt
4 large eggs, room temperature
1/2 lb unsalted butter, softened to room temperature
1 cup milk, room temperature
1-1/2 tsp coconut extract
2 limes (zest and juice)

Buttercream:
12 egg whites
1-1/2 cups granulated sugar
1-1/2 lbs unsalted butter, softened to room temperature
1 tsp coconut extract
2 limes (zest and juice)
3 cups sweet flaked coconut (garnish)

PREPARATION INSTRUCTIONS

Cake:

Sift cake flour, sugar, baking powder and salt in a mixing bowl. Add rest of the ingredients. Using a flat beater, mix at low speed for 20 seconds. Stop mixer. Scrape sides and bottom of bowl well. Resume beating at high speed for exactly two minutes. Pour into two prepared 9" or 10" baking pans and level the batter. Bake in 350°F oven for 25 to 35 minutes until toothpick inserted in center comes out clean. Cool on rack.

Buttercream:

Put egg whites and sugar in a mixing bowl over a double boiler and stir with a whisk until sugar is dissolved and is very warm (not hot). Remove from double boiler. Beat at high speed with wire beater until soft peaks form. Add butter, coconut extract and lime juice and beat until light and smooth (approximately 2 to 3 minutes). Frost bottom layer generously and dust with 1 cup flaked coconut. Apply top layer, frost top and sides, and dust with remaining coconut. Garnish with slices of fresh lime.

HELPFUL HINTS, VARIATIONS OR OTHER ADVICE

Make sure butter is at room temperature. If butter is completely melted cake will not rise.

ABOUT THE CHEF

Mark Brouillard is a self-taught pastry chef whose interest in baking began while his wife Jill was running a catering business in Rhode Island. His mother-in-law was quite the baker, although not professionally, and as he observed her his interest grew. Over the years he honed his skills, and after moving to Santa Barbara in 1988 he began working in various hotels as a waiter. In 1992 he became Pastry Chef at The Wine Cask Restaurant in Santa Barbara; he also sold wholesale pastries to area restaurants. In 1995 he and Jill opened Fresco Café. They are known today for their wonderful desserts.

THE STORY BEHIND THE RECIPE

When Jill was in high school she worked at a Howard Johnsons Restaurant. She had fond memories of a coconut cake there that she thought they made very well. Jill prodded Mark to make a cake similar to the one she remembered from her childhood.

FRESH Seafood Restaurant & Bar

1044 Wall Street
La Jolla, California 92037
858-551-7575
www.freshseafoodrestaurant.com

Coriander-Crusted Mahi Mahi
with Shrimp Risotto and Port Wine Reduction

By Chef Jeff Moogk

Serves 4

INGREDIENTS

4 oz butter
1/2 cup onion, minced
1 cup arborio rice
1 qt chicken stock
1/2 lb shrimp, cut in 1/4" pieces
3 oz butter

2 oz Parmesan, grated
1/4 cup chives, chopped
4 oz olive oil
4 Mahi filets, 6 oz each
1/2 cup coriander, ground
1 Tbs shallots, minced

2 cups Port wine
Salt and fresh ground white pepper,
  to taste
2 oz micro cilantro

PREPARATION INSTRUCTIONS

Risotto:

Begin by sweating onions in butter. Add in arborio rice and 1/3 of chicken stock. Stir rice constantly. When the stock is cooked out add another 1/3 of the stock. Continue to stir constantly. Season with salt and pepper.

Sauté shrimp in a separate sauté pan. Add cooked risotto and the last 1/3 of the chicken stock. Add Parmesan, butter and chives. Season to taste.

Mahi Mahi with Shrimp and Port Wine Reduction:

While rice is cooking, season Mahi filets with salt and pepper. Dredge one side in ground coriander. Heat olive oil in a large sauté pan. Place Mahi filets coriander-side down in the oil. Lightly brown coriander, flip once, and finish Mahi in the oven, crust-side down. Meanwhile, add shallots and Port wine to remaining oil in pan used to brown Mahi. Reduce to sauce consistency.

Plating:

Spoon risotto into the center of a round plate. Place a Mahi filet on top (coriander side up). Spoon Port wine reduction around. Garnish with micro cilantro.

ABOUT THE CHEF

As Executive Corporate Chef, Jeff Moogk oversees the sophisticated culinary operations of Ladeki Restaurant Group's fine dining venues, which include FRESH Seafood Restaurant & Bar. In addition to working closely with respective on-site executive chefs, he is continually developing and refining the innovative menus for 11 Sammy's Woodfired Pizza locations in California and Nevada. These responsibilities require not only a strong culinary background but substantial skills in management and human resources.

In designing menus, Moogk employs his fundamental culinary philosophy: "I think food should be fun…for both the customers and those preparing it," suggests the Executive Corporate Chef, adding, "I also try to turn people on to new ingredients and unfamiliar combinations of flavors or textures to enhance that sense of fun."

SUGGESTED WINE PAIRING

• 1997-2002 Kistler Chardonnay

Gourmet Get Togethers

Pash'e Culinary Professional Catering Group
The Santa Barbara Wine Train
The Radio Café

Pasadena, CA 91116
626-345-1816 310-270-7072

Lemon Chicken Pash'e™

By Chef Talli V. Counsel

Serves 4

INGREDIENTS

4 large lemons
4 bone-in chicken breasts with skin intact,
  seasoned to taste
2 Tbs extra virgin olive oil

1 tsp garlic, chopped
1 shallot, minced
1 tsp unsalted butter
Salt and pepper, to taste

PREPARATION INSTRUCTIONS

Squeeze the juice of two lemons over the chicken and allow to set for about 3 minutes. Season the chicken breasts with salt and pepper and return to refrigerator.

In a non-stick skillet, add two tablespoons of oil and heat on a low flame. Add garlic, shallot and zest of one lemon to the skillet. Wrap and set unused lemon aside to be used later. Slowly sauté and sweat the lemon zest, garlic and shallot until soft and translucent, about 10-15 minutes. This is to flavor the oil. Set the skillet aside and discard the sautéed items. Reserve the flavored oil in a bowl and set aside.

Return the skillet to the burner and add flavored oil and butter and set the burner at medium low heat. When oil is hot, place the pre-seasoned chicken breast skin side down and pan sear until skin is golden brown.

Turn off the flame and turn chicken breast over so it is skin side up. Place in a pre-heated 360°F oven for twelve minutes. Remove chicken from the oven and insert a thermometer. When the internal temperature reaches 150°F, remove it from the oven and squeeze the juice of the two remaining lemons over the skin side of the breast.

Reduce oven temperature to 340°F. Return skillet to the oven and continue to cook chicken until it reaches 165°F. Remove chicken from the oven and let rest for 5 minutes. Check temperature to make sure that it is 165°F before serving. Serve hot with sliced lemon and enjoy.

HELPFUL HINTS, VARIATIONS OR OTHER ADVICE

To get the most juice out of lemons, place them in a microwave for 10 seconds.

ABOUT THE CHEF

Chef Talli V. Counsel, M.B.A., C.M.C., Presidential Master Chef, is a native of Southern California. He was introduced to the culinary profession as a young man by his parents, who were chefs and owners of both Jean's Diner and Bill's Chicken In The Bag To Go, and Sugar Blue Catering in Pasadena, California, two of the most popular eateries of their time. Prior to his formal training at the culinary school of Olsen & Rogers, Chef Talli was fully trained in the art of high-speed "spincookery," a term developed by his mother, Chef Jean Counsel. In addition, Chef Talli is the Consulting Presidential Master Chef for two former United States Presidents.

The cuisines created by Chef Talli have garnered rave reviews. His broad culinary imagination and expertise, coupled with his unswerving commitment to using only the finest and freshest products from the best farmers and ranchers, have unleashed amazing American, international and fusion dishes, uniquely his own.

A few of his personally developed cuisines include: Italian Rainwater, European Crystal, Dr. Wooe's Chinese Hot Wok, California New Coastal Cuisine, Deep Gator Cajun Cuisine, and San Francisco Cable Cars & Crayons (extreme San Francisco flavors and colors). Other palate-pleasers include Americana Rail Cuisines and Blue Shadow Fresh Seafood, not to mention an array of the finest desserts, such as his award-winning White French Lemon Citronelle Cake and Paradise Macadamia Nut Cream Cake.

SUGGESTED WINE PAIRING

• Buttonwood Chardonnay

Grace Restaurant

GRACE
RESTAURANT

7360 Beverly Boulevard
Los Angeles, California 90036
323-934-4400
www.gracerestaurant.com

Dungeness Crab Salad with Peas, Mint and Meyer Lemon Vinaigrette

By Chef Neal Fraser

Serves 4

INGREDIENTS

8 oz Dungeness crab meat
2 oz frozen green peas
1/4 oz julienned mint
1/4 oz julienned Thai basil
1 oz mixed micro greens
Salt and pepper, to taste

Meyer Lemon Syrup:
1 cup Meyer lemon juice
1 cup sugar

Lemon Vinaigrette:
2 Meyer lemons (juiced)
4 oz lemon syrup (recipe above)
4 oz grapeseed oil
Rice wine vinegar

Basil Oil:
3 oz basil
3 oz grapeseed oil
Salt, to taste

PREPARATION INSTRUCTIONS

Meyer Lemon Syrup:

In medium saucepan, reduce by half to a sauce consistency. You will have more base than you need for this recipe.

Vinaigrette:

This vinaigrette is a little tricky because the acidity of the lemons will vary how much lemon juice and rice wine vinegar is necessary. You need to balance by taste. Add the 4 oz of lemon syrup, 4 oz of grapeseed oil and lemon juice. Add the rice wine vinegar to taste and balance with more oil if necessary.

Basil Oil:

Blanch basil in boiling salted water for 20 seconds and shock in ice water. Wring out water. In a blender, combine basil and grapeseed oil until puréed and add a touch of salt. Put purée in a stainless steel sauce pot and bring to a boil. Remove from heat and allow the purée to steep. Strain through a cheesecloth or chinois. Funnel the basil oil into a squirt bottle.

Salad Preparation:

Mix all dry ingredients except micro greens and season with vinaigrette. Season with salt and pepper and press into ring mold to form. Pack down and remove ring. Garnish top with micro greens. Garnish bowl with vinaigrette and basil oil.

ABOUT THE CHEF

Neal Fraser began his culinary career in Los Angeles at the age of 20, working as a line cook at Eureka Brewery and Restaurant, one of Wolfgang Puck's earliest restaurants. Fraser entered the Culinary Institute of America in Hyde Park, New York in the fall of 1990. During his tenure at the CIA, Fraser worked with such luminaries as Thomas Keller at the Checker's Hotel in Los Angeles and David Burke at the Park Avenue Café in New York. Upon returning to his native Los Angeles, Fraser continued cooking with the best in the business, including stretches at Joachim Splichal's Pinot Bistro, Wolfgang Puck's Spago and Hans Rockenwagner's Rox. Fraser opened Boxer in 1995 as Executive Chef and part-owner of the intimate 50 seat restaurant. After three years, Fraser moved on to Rix in Santa Monica. In the fall of 1999 Fraser took over the kitchens at the legendary Jimmy's in Beverly Hills. Due to a change in building ownership, Jimmy's closed it doors soon after Fraser's arrival. Neal Fraser spent his down time contemplating his next move: Grace Restaurant. As Partner and Executive Chef, Fraser serves his New American cuisine in an atmosphere perfectly designed to complement the ambitious flavors of one of Los Angeles' most revolutionary culinary talents.

SUGGESTED WINE PAIRING

• 2004 Sauvignon Blanc, New Zealand

THE STORY BEHIND THE RECIPE

This is a personal favorite that my opening Sous Chef and I came up with. It's fresh and clean with a ton of crab!

The Grill on the Alley

9560 Dayton Way
Beverly Hills, California 90210
310-276-0615
www.thegrill.com

Lobster Martini with Caviar

By Chef John Sola

Serves 6

INGREDIENTS

5 oz lobster meat mix (recipe below)
1 cup celery root remoulade
   (recipe below)
1 tsp black lumpfish caviar
2 lime wedges
Kosher salt, to taste

Lobster Meat Mix:
2 lbs Maine lobster meat
   (knuckles and claws)

1/2 cup Akvavit dressing
   (see recipe below)
1-1/2 Tbs lime juice

Celery Root Remoulade:
6 cups celery root
1/2 cup mayonnaise
1/2 cup sour cream
1/2 cup red onions, finely chopped
1/4 cup chives

Akvavit Dressing:
1 cup mayonnaise
1 cup sour cream
3 Tbs Akvavit liquor
1 tsp hot sauce
1 tsp lemon juice

PREPARATION INSTRUCTIONS

Lobster Meat Mix:
Combine lobster meat with dressing and lime juice.

Celery Root Remoulade:
Mix all the ingredients for the celery root remoulade together. It should not be wet-looking or feeling. Add kosher salt and hot sauce, to taste.

Akvavit Dressing:
Combine all ingredients for Akvavit dressing together in a bowl and mix until well blended. Salt, to taste.

Plating:
Place the celery root remoulade in an 8 oz martini glass. Add lobster meat mix on top of remoulade, then top with the caviar. Place a lime wedge half-way down the glass and serve another wedge with a cocktail fork.

ABOUT THE CHEF

Executive Chef John Sola is the master craftsman behind Grill Concepts' straightforward classic American cuisine. Together with Bob Spivak, President of Grill Concepts, he created the menu responsible for the restaurant group's immediate and continued success. Prior to joining the Grill, Sola was the protegé of Rolph Nonnast (who formerly worked under Ken Hansen at Scandia) at the Chronicle Restaurant located on Main Street in Santa Monica from 1979-1982. There Sola acquired extensive operations experience and honed the skills that helped him evolve into the highly respected Executive Chef that he is today. Sola began his culinary career in Stateline, Nevada at the age of 20 as a prep cook for Harrah's Hotel & Casino. His talent was quickly recognized and he was promoted to head Saucier at the property's French restaurant, The Summit. More than three years of experience at Harrah's exposed him to the hotel's eclectic mix of restaurants, which included Chinese, a steakhouse and a seafood bar. After leaving Harrah's in 1976, Sola became Executive Chef of Heavenly Valley Ski Resort in South Lake Tahoe. Three years later he joined The Chronicle, and after three and a half years he was asked by Bob Spivak to help create The Grill. In the Summer of 2001, Sola was given the title of Vice President of Operations & Development for Grill Concepts, Inc., and in 2004 he was given the title of Senior Vice President, Culinary. In addition to his role of Executive Chef, Sola now oversees the operations of the company's 20-plus restaurants and the development of all the company's future endeavors.

Hugo's Restaurant

8401 Santa Monica Boulevard
West Hollywood, CA 90069-4209
323-654-3993

12851 Riverside Drive
Studio City, California 91607
818-761-8985
www.hugosrestaurant.com

Pasta Mama

By Owner Tom Kaplan

Serves 1

INGREDIENTS

5 oz (about 1/3 lb) cooked linguine (or spaghetti)
1 Tbs butter, oil or margarine
1 tsp garlic, chopped
2 Tbs onion, chopped
2 Tbs parsley, chopped

1/2 tsp seasoning salt (or to taste)
Pinch ground pepper
2 extra large eggs, beaten
1 Tbs Parmesan cheese, grated

PREPARATION INSTRUCTIONS

Cook pasta according to directions on box. Fresh pasta takes 2-3 minutes. Melt butter in a sauté pan over medium heat. Add garlic, onion, parsley and seasoning and sauté for 1-2 minutes. Add cooked pasta, mix with seasoning and stir until well coated. Add eggs, mixing well with pasta. Just before eggs are cooked through, mix in cheese.

HELPFUL HINTS, VARIATIONS OR OTHER ADVICE

This dish is easily increased for more than one person and has multiple variations, as we've discovered over the years. You can add bacon, sausage or chicken. You can add any vegetable you would put in an omelet. If you start with cooked pasta from the night before, make sure you warm it through before adding eggs. Even though this is an easy brunch dish, we serve Pasta Mama all day long.

ABOUT THE OWNER

Tom Kaplan has been in the restaurant business over 25 years, starting at Hugo's with his father, Terry Kaplan. He opened Caffe Latte with his wife, Emily, and eventually opened a coffeehouse in 1990, Highland Grounds. He returned to Hugo's in the late '90's when his dad retired, and opened a second Hugo's in the summer of 2000 which was recently named the Best Breakfast Place in Los Angeles by CitiSearch.com. Last year saw the opening of Hugo's Tacos, kitty-corner from Hugo's Restaurant on Riverside and Coldwater in the Valley. Hugo's chef of approximately ten years is Nabor Diaz.

SUGGESTED BEVERAGE PAIRING

- As this is primarily a breakfast dish, rich and hearty, a wonderfully crisp and acidic juice or tea would work well. I'd suggest our citrus-y Green Juice made with fresh orange juice, banana, Rice Bran syrup, almond oil and liquid chlorophyll.

- For a tea recommendation, Tieguanyin Oolong would work well. This award-winning tea is lightly oxidized for an oolong, while retaining some of the crisp, acidic qualities of a green tea. Both beverages would hold up well to the garlic, eggs and pasta dish.

THE STORY BEHIND THE RECIPE

Pasta Mama originated as a dish Mom used to make for us kids using leftover spaghetti from the night before. When Dad and I were deciding in the early '80's whether we should keep Hugo's open for breakfast or open later in the day, he said to me, "Why don't you focus as much energy on breakfast as other restaurants do on dinner?" That's when I thought, "We've got fresh pasta," and I put the dish together the way I remembered it and added it to our menu. Within weeks, we became known as the home of the "Power Breakfast" and there were Steven Spielberg, John Landis and George Lucas all sitting around a table together. Of course, Dad always said, "Love is our greatest power," and we think that's the biggest reason we've been in business for over 30 years (we think we've got great food, too!). We try to impart to our staff and customers the real meaning of hospitality.

Inn of the Seventh Ray

128 Old Topanga Canyon Road
Topanga, California 90290
310-455-1311
www.innoftheseventhray.com

Pan-Roasted Halibut with Wilted Butter Lettuce, Fresh Spring Peas and Pine Nuts

By Chef Daniel Holzman

Serves 4

INGREDIENTS

4 (7-oz) fillets of fresh halibut
1/2 cup olive oil
1 cup spring peas, blanched in salty boiling water for 1 minute
1 head butter lettuce, washed and roughly cut into 1" strips

Pine Nut Sauce:
1 cup stale bread, torn and soaked in water
3/8 cup pine nuts
1/2 cup olive oil
Juice of 2 lemons
1/2 cup chopped garlic
2 pinches kosher salt

Bagna Cauda:
3/4 cup olive oil
1-1/2 cloves garlic
3/8 cup pine nuts
Zest of 2 lemons

PREPARATION INSTRUCTIONS

Pine Nut Sauce:

In a blender combine soaked stale bread (drain any excess water but do not squeeze), half the pine nuts, 1/2 cup of olive oil, the juice of two lemons, 1/2 cup chopped garlic and two pinches of kosher salt. Blend until smooth, adding water as necessary. Hold over a low flame to warm.

Bagna Cauda:

Over medium heat warm 3/4 cup of olive oil with the remaining 1-1/2 cloves of garlic until just bubbling. Add 3/8 cup pine nuts and the lemon zest. Remove from heat and let sit.

Halibut:

Pre-heat oven to 450°F. Season halibut fillets generously with kosher salt and pat dry. In a large sauté pan, with plenty of room for all of the fish, heat 1/4 cup olive oil over a high flame until it begins to smoke. Momentarily remove the pan from the heat to avoid splattering and gently place the fillets into the pan. Immediately return pan to heat and let cook for one and a half minutes. Put pan in the oven to continue cooking for three to four minutes. In the meantime, heat another medium large pan with the remaining oil. Once a drop of water sizzles, add butter lettuce, peas and a pinch of salt. Sauté until wilted, about two minutes. Distribute vegetables evenly in the center of four plates. Ladle pine nut sauce around. Remove the fish from the oven and carefully flip each fillet onto the center of the plate, golden brown side up. Generously spoon the bagna cauda over the fish and around the plate.

ABOUT THE CHEF

Daniel Holzman began cooking professionally at the age of thirteen under the tutelage of Chef Eric Ripert at his flagship four-star restaurant, Le Bernardin, in New York City.

At Chef Ripert's direction Daniel attended the Culinary Institute of America while continuing his work at Le Bernardin on weekends and during the holidays. Later, Daniel served under the late, esteemed chef Jean Louis Palladin at both Napa restaurant in Las Vegas and while opening his Palladin in New York City. Moving to San Francisco, Daniel worked under Laurant Manrique at the Campton Place Hotel and later with Laurant Gras at the Fifth Floor in the Hotel Palomar. Daniel comes to us by way of AXE restaurant in Venice, California where he served as chef until December of 2005.

HELPFUL HINTS, VARIATIONS OR OTHER ADVICE

Be patient, that's what it's all about! If the fish sticks, it's just not ready to come out. Put it back on the fire and check it again in a minute or two.

SUGGESTED WINE PAIRING

• Any dry white wine

J. Taylor's Restaurant

1540 Camino Del Mar
Del Mar, California 92014
858-793-6442
www.laubergedelmar.com

Boneless Rack of Colorado Lamb, Goat Cheese Gratin, Spiced Pepper Jam, Smoked Tomato-Rosemary Glacé

By Chef Paul McCabe

Serves 4

INGREDIENTS

Lamb:
2 racks Colorado lamb
2 Tbs garlic, chopped
2 sprigs fresh thyme
1/4 cup extra virgin olive oil
2 cup brioche crumbs
2 Tbs chervil, chopped

Goat Cheese Gratin:
11 oz goat cheese
16 oz heavy cream
2 Tbs garlic, minced

2 Tbs shallots, minced
1 Tbs thyme, chopped
1 Tbs chives, chopped
2 Tbs parsley, chopped
4 Yukon Gold potatoes
Salt and pepper

Black Pepper Tomato Jam:
1-1/2 cup tomato, peeled, seeded and chopped small
Zest of 1/2 lemon
Juice of 1 lemon

1/4 tsp allspice, ground
1/4 tsp cloves, ground
3-1/2 oz sugar
1 Tbs black pepper, ground
1 Tbs parsley, chopped
1/3 cup onion, sliced thin
1 Tbs powdered fruit pectin

Smoked Tomato-Rosemary Glacé:
8 cloves garlic, sliced
5 shallots, sliced

3 cups good red wine
4 Roma tomatoes, deseeded
1-1/2 gal veal stock
Reserved lamb bones, roasted to a golden brown
2 sprigs thyme
4 sprigs rosemary
2 cup mesquite chips

PREPARATION INSTRUCTIONS

Lamb: Remove the fat cap and silver skin from both racks. Cut each rack in half, leaving four bones per portion. Remove all the bones except the one on the end and reserve for the sauce. Marinate the lamb in oil, garlic and thyme for at least six hours. Combine the brioche and chervil and set aside. Remove the lamb from the marinade and season with salt and pepper. Sear the lamb on all sides then wrap the bone with aluminum foil. Coat the lamb with bread crumb mixture and roast in a 400°F oven for 10 to 15 minutes. Remove the foil and let rest for at least 7 minutes.

Gratin: Combine cream, garlic, shallots and herbs in mixing bowl and season liberally with salt and pepper. Slice the potatoes 1/8" thick and place directly into the cream mixture. Layer a greased pan with the potatoes and goat cheese and repeat until all potatoes and cheese are used. Drain excess cream. Cover with foil and bake at 350°F for 25 to 35 minutes. Remove the cover and bake until golden brown. Let rest at room temperature.

Jam: In a saucepan combine everything except the pectin and slowly bring to a simmer. Add pectin to dissolve, remove from heat and cool until set.

(cont'd)

ABOUT THE CHEF

Acclaimed local chef Paul McCabe is making a splash in Del Mar as the new Executive Chef of the romantic L'Auberge Del Mar Resort and Spa and J.Taylor's Restaurant. Formerly at Top of the Cove and Star of the Sea, trend-setting Chef McCabe is heralded as one of the "Rising Stars of American Cuisine" by the James Beard Foundation. McCabe has cooked for some of Hollywood's most revered stars including Gwyneth Paltrow, Robert DeNiro, Eddie Murphy and Al Pacino. He is recognized as a Chef Rotisseur by the prestigious French dining association, the Chaine de Rotisseurs. McCabe's cuisine has been featured in *The New York Times*, *The Los Angeles Times*, *The San Diego Union Tribune* and on the Discovery Channel and the Food Network. You'll find diverse styles of food at J.Taylor's…but never intermingled in one dish. Instead you will find American regional ingredients reminiscent of a single culture's fare. Breathtakingly pure flavors in unexpected juxtapositions—never layered, masked or overly adorned.

PREPARATION INSTRUCTIONS
(cont'd)

Glacé: In a saucepot over medium-low heat, sauté the garlic and shallots until caramelized. Add wine and reduce by three-quarters. Place the wood chips in a baking pan and the tomatoes on perforated pan and set over the chips. Cover with foil, place on a burner over medium heat and smoke for 10 minutes. Set aside. Add the veal stock and bones to the reduced wine and bring to a simmer. At this stage it is very important to skim all impurities that rise to the surface. Reduce by half. When the lamb bones separate from each other strain the sauce. Place the sauce into a smaller pot, add the smoked tomatoes, skim and reduce by one quarter. The sauce is ready when it coats the back of a spoon. Add thyme and rosemary and steep for 5 minutes. Strain, season and reserve.

Presentation: Sauté some red swiss chard and place on the plates. Slice the lamb into five pieces and shingle it with the bone resting on the chard. With a round cutter, cut out the gratin and place it to the right of the lamb and place a tablespoon of the jam in the lower right corner. Top the lamb with sauce, sprinkle with fleur de sel and serve.

SUGGESTED WINE PAIRING

• 2003 Masut Pinot Noir, Redwood Valley

Jack n' Jill's of Beverly Hills

342 North Beverly Drive
Beverly Hills, California 90210
310-247-4500
www.eatatjacknjills.com

Savannah Strawberry-Oatmeal Pancakes

By Chef Robert A. Benson

Serves 6

INGREDIENTS

2 cups rolled oats
2 cups buttermilk
1/2 cup flour
4 eggs
2 Tbs sugar
1 tsp baking powder

1 tsp baking soda
1/2 tsp kosher salt
15 fresh medium sized strawberries, sliced

Powdered sugar, butter and maple syrup, to taste

PREPARATION INSTRUCTIONS

In a mixing bowl, let rolled oats soak in buttermilk for 15 minutes. Add rest of ingredients (except strawberries), stirring gently until mixed and all dry products have been incorporated. Do not overmix. Spoon on a slightly greased griddle or non-stick pan at 350ºF. Add 4-5 sliced strawberries to each cake. Pancakes will be thick and will take 2-3 minutes per side to cook. Garnish with fresh strawberries and powdered sugar.

HELPFUL HINTS, VARIATIONS OR OTHER ADVICE

Don't overmix. For fluffier cakes with better color, let the batter sit at room temperature for 5-10 minutes before using. Optional: Serve with butter and maple syrup on side.

ABOUT THE CHEF

Robert A. Benson is a New Orleans-born restaurant owner/chef who brings a southern flavor to Beverly Hills. Robert has had over 20 years of restaurant experience and has restaurants in Beverly Hills and Santa Monica, CA.

THE STORY BEHIND THE RECIPE

This is one of my personal favorite recipes. It is a nice break from ordinary pancakes and fresh off the griddle, the smells remind me of Sunday.

Joan's on Third

8350 West Third Street
Los Angeles, California 90048
323-655-2285
www.joansonthird.com

Joan's Macaroni & Cheese

By Chef Joan McNamara

Serves 10

INGREDIENTS

1 lb pasta (elbow macaroni, fusilli, or any shape desired)
2 oz butter
3-3/4 cups whole milk
6 oz ricotta or small curd cottage cheese
3 oz cream cheese

12 oz Monterey Jack, shredded
20 oz Old Amsterdam Gouda, shredded
  (save 8 oz for topping)
Salt and pepper, to taste

PREPARATION INSTRUCTIONS

Preheat oven to 350°F. Cook pasta in large pot of boiling, salted water until just tender. Drain well. Add butter, milk, ricotta, cream cheese, monterey jack and 12 oz of the Gouda to the warm pasta. Season with salt and pepper. Gently mix everything together, leaving some chunks of cheese visible. Pour the mixture into 9 x 11-inch baking pan. Top with the remaining 8 oz of Gouda. Bake until beautifully golden, 30-40 minutes. Serve hot or room temperature. Enjoy!

ABOUT THE CHEF

Joan McNamara grew up in Manhattan and in Europe where, at the tender age of 7, she first discovered her passion for cooking. Though she was barely tall enough to see what creation she and her mom were making, Joan had found her calling. Over the years, as she grew and her talents for cuisine increased, so did her desire to share her unique and yet familiar flavors with the public. Thus, Joan's on Third was cooked up out of this dream. Fortunately for Joan, her two entrepreneurial daughters have inherited this passion and have followed in the tradition of their Mom with Susie who runs the gourmet foods marketplace and Carol as the Director of Special Events and Catering. With the family working together, Joan's on Third continues to grow and has become a food emporium known for culinary delights ranging from Turkey Meatloaf with Chili Aioli to Macaroni & Cheese, decadent Lemon Bars and Cupcakes.

THE STORY BEHIND THE RECIPE

Joan's Macaroni & Cheese is her mother's recipe that Joan grew up eating.

Johnny Garlic's California Pasta Grill

8988 Brooks Road South
Windsor, California 95492
707-328-4018
www.johnnygarlics.com

CALIFORNIA
Restaurant
ASSOCIATION
CELEBRATING 100 YEARS OF SERVICE
1906-2006

Chipotle Pasta

By Chef Guy Fieri

Serves 4

INGREDIENTS

1 oz olive oil
1 hot link sausage, cut in
  6 bias slices
1/4 lb (21/25) shrimp, deveined,
  shelled and butterflied
4 oz heavy cream
3 oz chipotle sauce
1/2 tsp sea salt
1/2 tsp ground black pepper
9 oz cooked penne pasta
2 oz Parmesan cheese, grated

Garnish:
1 tsp tomato, diced
1 tsp scallion, diced

Chipotle Sauce:
1 cup BBQ sauce
1/2 cup canola oil
1/4 cup lemon juice
1/2 oz Dijon mustard
2 oz chipotle paste
1/2 oz red chili flakes
1/4 tsp cayenne pepper
1/4 tsp ground black pepper

PREPARATION INSTRUCTIONS

Chipotle Sauce:

Combine all sauce ingredients in blender, purée, cover and refrigerate.

Chipotle Pasta:

In sauté pan over high heat, add olive oil and hot links. Sear links until browned. Add the shrimp and cook until pink. Lower heat to medium. Add cream, chipotle sauce, salt and pepper. Add cooked pasta and cheese. Toss to combine.

Plating:

Serve in pasta bowl and garnish with diced tomato, scallions and more grated Parmesan.

ABOUT THE CHEF

Guy "Guido" Fieri was born and raised in Northern California. His food career began at age ten selling soft pretzels from his homemade three-wheeled bicycle cart. By age sixteen Guy had earned enough money from selling pretzels and washing dishes to take a one-year trip to France. Upon returning to the United States, Guy continued his formal foodservice education. Guy graduated in 1990 from the University of Nevada Las Vegas with a B.S. in Hospitality Management and went to work for Stouffer Restaurants, then Louise's Trattoria. At Louise's, he met Steven Gruber. In 1996 the two opened their own concept, Johnny Garlic's California Pasta Grill. In the ensuing ten years they opened two more Johnny Garlic's, a catering division, Tex Wasabi's and Russell Ramsay's Chop House. He currently serves on the Board of Directors for the Educational Foundation of the California Restaurant Association. Guy recently won the Food Network's "The Next Food Network Star" and is currently filming his own show. Guy lives in Santa Rosa, California, with his beloved Lori, and their two sons, Hunter, 9, and new baby Ryder.

THE STORY BEHIND THE RECIPE

Johnny Garlic's is one of our three restaurant concepts (also Tex Wasabi's and Russell Ramsay's Chop House). We call ourselves a California Pasta Grill, featuring unique twists on pastas, steaks and seafood. The Chipotle pepper, a smoked jalapeno, is so often only found in Mexican dishes, but when added to a traditional Parmesan alfredo and enhanced with some Louisiana hot links and some prawns it turns into a multi-cultural food fest. We love to work with items like the chipotle, and this dish will make you a fan as well.

Kellogg West

3801 West Temple Avenue
Pomona, California 91768
909-860-4876
www.kelloggwest.org

BBQ Duck and Three-Pepper Burrito

By Chef Andy Abelman

Serves 4

INGREDIENTS

2 (10-12 oz) duck breasts
2 red peppers
2 green peppers
2 yellow peppers
1 large white onion

4 Tbs olive oil
2 cups BBQ sauce
4 8" flour tortillas
8 slices spiced jack cheese
Salt and pepper, to taste

PREPARATION INSTRUCTIONS

Score skin of duck breasts and salt and pepper lightly. Place in 360°F oven for 15 minutes. Julienne peppers into 3" x 1/4" slices. Put aside one strip of each pepper for plate garnish. Slice onion approximately same size as peppers. In large skillet, sauté onions in olive oil until translucent. Add peppers and sauté until cooked but still slightly crisp. Remove skin and slice duck breast to same size as peppers. Add duck breasts to skillet and cook for approximately five minutes. Add BBQ sauce to skillet and cook on medium heat until BBQ sauce is slightly bubbling.

Take a tortilla and fill middle with duck, pepper and onion mixture. Fold over one side and then the other to form a burrito. Place on sheet pan and top with two slices of spiced jack cheese. Place in broiler until cheese is golden brown. Remove and cut in half. Plate with one half over the other half. Garnish with BBQ sauce on plate and diced three color peppers around rim.

HELPFUL HINTS, VARIATIONS OR OTHER ADVICE

For a nice variation, add mango purée and orange juice to your BBQ sauce for a tropical flare.

ABOUT THE CHEF

A hospitality professional for over 30 years, Andy's primary responsibility is as General Manager of Kellogg West Conference Center & Lodge, located on the grounds of Cal Poly Pomona University. Additional responsibilities include overseeing the culinary program for the operation and assisting with all high-end events on campus including dinners at the house of the President of the University.

SUGGESTED WINE PAIRING

- Any good Sauvignon Blanc or Pinot Gris works well with the dish. I like 2003 Cakebread Sauvignon Blanc.

THE STORY BEHIND THE RECIPE

This recipe is one I created nearly fifteen years ago with my chef when I was managing a hotel in Hawaii. I came up with the recipe and my chef then eventually worked out a BBQ sauce, for which he won an award. We then had the sauce bottled, and sold it in our gift shops. Since then, I have used this recipe at every property I have been at and it is a favorite for all that have it. I hope everyone enjoys it as much as we have.

LAC+USC Medical Center

1200 North State Street
Los Angeles, California 90033
323-226-6901
www.ladhs.org

Grilled Mahi Mahi with Orange Coconut Sauce

By Chef Stephen Puccini

Serves 4

INGREDIENTS

4 Mahi Mahi filets
1 Tbs olive oil
Salt and pepper, to taste

Orange Coconut Sauce:
2 cups orange juice
1/4 cup coconut milk

1 Tbs soy sauce
1 Tbs puréed candied ginger
7 black peppercorns
6 Tbs unsalted butter, cut into chunks and chilled
1/4 cups fresh chives, cut 1/8" thick

PREPARATION INSTRUCTIONS

Prepare grill for cooking with direct heat. Rub Mahi Mahi filets with olive oil and season with salt and pepper. Grill Mahi Mahi over medium high heat, 3-4 minutes per side.

Orange Coconut Sauce:

Combine orange juice, coconut milk, soy sauce, candied ginger purée and peppercorns in a small saucepan and reduce by 2/3 while simmering over low heat. Strain and keep warm. Prior to serving, whisk in butter, one piece at a time. Spoon over Mahi Mahi and garnish with chopped chives.

HELPFUL HINTS, VARIATIONS OR OTHER ADVICE

Any firm fish such as halibut or salmon will work. This dish goes extremely well with a coconut rice pilaf.

ABOUT THE CHEF

While immersed in cooking at an early age due to a restaurant-owning family, Stephen Puccini has only recently entered the professional culinary world. He attended the Scottsdale Culinary Institute in Arizona, from which he graduated in 2002. Stephen has worked for Marriott hotels as well as several restaurants and corporate dining rooms in the Phoenix area prior to returning to California. When not cooking in the hectic atmosphere of a large production kitchen, he relaxes by cooking in his own laid-back kitchen for his wife Lisa and his son and daughter.

SUGGESTED WINE PAIRING

- 2003 Simi Russian River Reserve Chardonnay

THE STORY BEHIND THE RECIPE

This recipe was developed while trying to create a healthier sauce for grilled fish. The juice reduction is quite flavorful, but the addition of the butter really brings it all together. This is a favorite in the Puccini household.

L'Escale

2000 Second Street
Coronado, California 92118
619-438-1910
www.lescale.signonsandiego.com

Delicata Squash Gratin with Figs and Boule d'Or

By Chef Ladan Raissi

Serves 4

INGREDIENTS

2 tsp chopped garlic

1 tsp chopped fresh thyme

1 lb delicata squash, peeled, seeds removed and cut into 1/4" slices

1 lb Yukon Gold potatoes, peeled and cut into 1/4" slices

Kosher salt

Fresh ground pepper

1 cup heavy cream

1/2 cup sliced dried figs

1/2 cup Boule D'Or cheese (mimolette), shredded or shaved

1/2 cup creme fraiche

2 egg yolks

1/4 tsp nutmeg

4 oz petite arugula

1 Tbs toasted pumpkin seeds

PREPARATION INSTRUCTIONS

Preheat oven to 350°F. Butter an 8" X 8" pan, add chopped thyme and garlic. Put the squash slices and potato in a large bowl and season with salt and pepper. Add heavy cream and toss, incorporating cream into the squash and potatoes. Arrange 1/2 the squash slices and 1/2 the potatoes at the bottom of the baking dish and season. Top with figs in a single layer. Add cheese, sprinkle with half the garlic and thyme. Then cover with remaining squash and potatoes, sprinkle with remaining garlic and thyme. Cover with foil and bake 45 minutes, or until tender. Remove. Whisk together crème fraiche, egg yolks and nutmeg. Season to taste and spread over gratin evenly. Bake uncovered until golden, 5-10 minutes. Remove and let rest for 10 minutes before serving. To serve: Cut into rounds and top with petite arugula and toasted pumpkin seeds.

HELPFUL HINTS, VARIATIONS OR OTHER ADVICE

You can substitute butternut squash or any type of rich sweet winter squash. Instead of figs, you can use dried apricots. This is a unique side dish to serve at Thanksgiving. It pairs well with poultry, lamb and my personal favorite: roasted duck breast and pomegranate sauce.

SUGGESTED WINE PAIRING

• 2001 Fiddlehead Lollapalooza Fiddlestix Pinot Noir, Santa Ynez Valley

THE STORY BEHIND THE RECIPE

The inspiration for this recipe was a salad I had made using slices of roasted delicata squash and the French cheese, Boule d'Or. The combination of the salty cheese and sweet squash was fantastic, so I decided to pair them in a gratin. It is also a great seasonal dish, and made its debut on my autumn menu.

ABOUT THE CHEF

Cooking was always a design for life for Ladan Raissi. Her father was an entrepreneurial giant, the "Pizza King" of Iran, and a maverick in the restaurant world, opening the first fast food franchise in the Middle East. He entertained the Shah and celebrities in his restaurants, while Ladan herself grew up among the aromas in the buzz of activity and excitement of the restaurant world. She trained at the Natural Gourmet Culinary School and Institute for Food and Health in New York City. Specializing in the properties and preparation of whole foods and indigenous cooking methods, she has made it her mission to use fresh, seasonal and organic ingredients while combining abstract flavors. She spent a year in the South of France learning about regional wines and provincial cuisine. Having worked at the notable Beard House in New York and having sailed around the Caribbean as a private chef on a yacht, Ladan brings together the traditional flavors of other cultures with a fresh twist on cosmopolitan cuisine. Her dishes maintain the vitality of fresh garden ingredients reminiscent of Ladan's Persian heritage.

Locanda del Lago

231 Arizona Avenue
Santa Monica, California 90401
310-451-3525
www.LagoSantaMonica.com

Ossobuco Alla Milanese
(Veal Shanks with Saffron Risotto)

By Chef Davide Vedovelli

Serves 4

INGREDIENTS

Ossobuco:
4 veal shanks (1 lb each)
2 onions, finely chopped
3 carrots, finely chopped
4 celery stalks, finely chopped
4 bay leaves
2/3 cup extra virgin olive oil
1/2 cup flour
1 cup dry white wine
16 oz vine-ripened plum tomatoes or canned
   Italian plum tomatoes
2 cups veal broth
Salt and white pepper, to taste

Risotto:
3 cups chicken stock
1/2 Tbs saffron
1/3 cup extra virgin olive oil
1 Tbs onion, finely chopped
1 cup arborio rice, "riso arborio superfino" (8 oz)
1/2 cup dry white wine
1 Tbs butter
2 Tbs grated Parmesan cheese

PREPARATION INSTRUCTIONS

Ossobuco:

Pre-heat a roasting pan over medium heat with 1/3 cup olive oil. Sweat the chopped onions, celery and carrots (keeping 1 Tbs of chopped onion aside for the risotto) in the oil with the bay leaves until the onion and the celery are translucent. Pre-heat a sauce pan over medium-high heat with 1/3 cup olive oil. Lightly coat the veal shanks in the flour. Sear for 4-5 minutes on each side, adding salt and pepper to both sides. Place the veal shanks in the roasting pan, carefully arranging them on top of the brunoise of vegetables. Add 1 cup white wine and simmer until the wine evaporates, turning veal shanks over halfway through in order to flavor both sides with the wine and vegetables. Finely chop the plum tomatoes and add, along with their juice, to the roasting pan. Add the veal broth, bring to a boil and season to taste. Cover and place in an oven pre-heated to 350°F. Cooking time is approximately three hours. Be sure to turn the veal shanks over every 20 minutes so they can absorb the flavors. Also, ensure that the shanks are at least half covered by liquid, adding more veal broth if necessary. When finished, the meat should be very tender. If the sauce becomes thick, add additional veal broth to obtain proper consistency.

Risotto:

When the ossobuco has been cooking for 2-1/2 hours, start preparing the risotto. Bring the chicken stock and saffron up to a boil in a sauce pan. Reduce heat and simmer. Place another sauce pan over medium heat and add 1/3 cup olive oil. Sweat 1 Tbs of chopped onion until translucent and add the arborio rice. Stir the rice with a wooden spoon for one minute,

(cont'd)

ABOUT THE CHEF

Executive Chef Davide Vedovelli joined Locanda del Lago in 2003 with impressive credentials as Sous Chef at Savini, one of Milan's top restaurants, and chef at Cestino, another top Milan restaurant whose reputation for authentic Milanese cuisine was built by Vedovelli. Vedovelli arrived at Lago from Italy after two years as chef at Bellagio's Trattoria San Giacomo, which was named "Best Trattoria" in a *Los Angeles Times* feature story on Italy's Lake Region. Also a bread-making, pastry and pasta artisan, Vedovelli owned a store called Pasta Fresca, which sold fresh, hand-made pasta to the public and the restaurant trade for nine years. He was also a chef at Regina Palace, a five-star hotel in Stresa, at Restaurant Rozal, a high-end Hungarian restaurant in Milan, and at Mario in London, among others. Vedovelli was born into a family of restaurateurs who owned an establishment in the Emilia region that was 160 years old. He began his career at age 14 at a cooking school in Milan and apprenticed at the five-star Leonardo da Vinci Hotel as well as the five-star hotel La Tour de Super Crans in Switzerland.

PREPARATION INSTRUCTIONS
(cont'd)

then add 1/2 cup of white wine and stir constantly until completely absorbed. Turn the heat to low and pour one ladle of chicken-saffron broth into the rice pan while constantly stirring. As the liquid is absorbed by the rice, continue adding broth, ladle by ladle, and stir until the rice grain has at least doubled in volume. Test rice grain for softness and when ready (approximately 20-25 minutes), add butter and Parmesan cheese, remove from heat and stir to creamy consistency. To plate, place the saffron risotto on one side and the veal shank adjacent. Pour the sauce over the shank and serve steaming hot.

THE STORY BEHIND THE RECIPE

Lago's co-owner West Hooker says, "Ossobuco alla Milanese is one of the most representative dishes of Milano, a region that we focus on at Lago, and Ossobuco alla Milanese is among my favorite dishes of all. It has been on our menu for many years. When living in Milano, one of my favorite treats was going to a restaurant to have the perfect ossobuco accompanied by the perfect saffron risotto. I still feel the same today."

Lucia and Company

P.O. Box 91205
Long Beach, California 90804
562-397-4249
www.LuciaAndCompany.com

Mexican Chocolate Bread Pudding with Kahlúa

By Chef Lucia E. Robles

Serves 16

INGREDIENTS

9 egg yolks
2-1/2 cups sugar, packed
2-1/4 cups milk
2-1/4 cups cream

1/4 tsp vanilla extract
1/2 cup Kahlúa
1 lb loaf cinnamon bread, cubed
3 tablets Ibarra Mexican chocolate, broken into pieces

PREPARATION INSTRUCTIONS

With a whisk mix yolks and sugar together until pale yellow. Boil milk and cream. Slowly combine milk with egg and sugar mixture. Add in the vanilla extract and the Kahlúa. In a large bowl toss the bread with the milk, egg and Kahlúa mixture and let stand for 30 minutes. If necessary, allow it to soak longer to ensure the bread is soggy but not to the point of losing its shape. Spray a 10" x 14" pan with a non-stick baking spray. Gently place bread mixture into pan. Place the chocolate pieces evenly on top, pressing down into bread mixture to prevent burning.

Bake at 275°F until a knife inserted into center of pan comes out clean, approximately 30 - 45 minutes. This dessert is best after it has set for a day in the refrigerator, although it can be enjoyed as soon as it has cooled. Either way, serve with a dollop of whipped cream and a sprig of mint. Enjoy!

HELPFUL HINTS, VARIATIONS OR OTHER ADVICE

Although it may seem like a lot of liquid at the time, the custard should be completely absorbed by the bread during the baking process. For best results refrigerate for a day. A good heavy, dense bread should be used for this dessert; light and fluffy loaves do not work well for this recipe. If made correctly, this dessert should come out moist, not on the drier side like most bread puddings.

ABOUT THE CHEF

After a lifelong love affair with food, eating and feeding others, Lucia finally decided to make her fantasy a reality and attend culinary school. She enrolled in the California School of Culinary Arts, Le Cordon Bleu Program in Pasadena, California. Her education focused on classic French culinary traditions and techniques. She graduated at the top of her class, on the Dean's list and with a Perfect Attendance Award. Lucia worked in local restaurants and hotels before founding her own catering company, Lucia and Company, in 2004. Of the hours that can go into preparing one dish Lucia says, "The joy in cooking for someone else is watching sheer bliss overcome them as they take their first bite. It makes everything worthwhile."

SUGGESTED BEVERAGE PAIRING

- 1 part Bailey's Irish Cream, 1 Part Kahlúa, 1 Part + an extra splash of Frangelico, served over ice.

THE STORY BEHIND THE RECIPE

The inspiration for this recipe came from my love of Mexican chocolate (okay, my mom's obsession with chocolate and my dad's love of Mexican-style bread puddings), the desire to make a truly delicious dessert and the need to add liquor to everything! Not being a big fan of bread puddings in general, I wanted something that I could truly enjoy with my family that is easy to put together.

The Main Event by Melody

9147 Hazeltine Avenue
Panorama City, California 91402
973-326-9461
www.showbizchef.com

Thanksgiving Stuffing...from our WOR Radio 710 Thanksgiving Feast

By Chef Melody McGinley Whitelaw

Serves 10

INGREDIENTS

2 cups celery, sliced
1 lb mushrooms, sliced and browned
2 cups onions, minced
1 lb pork or turkey sausage, browned
12 cups bread cubes, toasted (Rubschlager sour-dough, wheat, pumpernickle and homemade corn bread)
1 small can water chestnuts
1 can black olives, sliced in half

3 red peppers, grilled and sliced thin
1/2 cup chopped fresh parsley
1/4 cup chopped fresh dill
2 tsp sage
Olive oil spray
4 14-oz cans chicken broth
2 sticks butter, melted
Salt and pepper, to taste

PREPARATION INSTRUCTIONS

Lightly brown celery, mushrooms and onions. Brown sausage and break up. Add bread cubes, rest of vegetables, herbs, butter and broth. Lightly mix, adding more broth as needed. Bake in casserole pan sprayed with olive oil, 45 minutes covered, 15 minutes uncovered.

ABOUT THE CHEF

Melody McGinley Whitelaw is the owner of The Main Event by Melody. Her father, Norman McGinley, was an early film caterer from his taverns in Los Angeles. She was taught to cook at the knee of her father and grandmothers. She feels blessed to have grown up around such wonderful cooks. She went to Valley College where she learned her passion for cooking from Professor Ida Jaqua, with whom she remains close friends. She then attended UCLA to study nutrition. The Main Event has been in business for over forty years. Chef Melody is currently a guest chef at Bloomingdales and Macy*s in Herald Square in New York City. She has been a guest chef on WOR Radio 710 NYC for the past 15 years where she can be heard on the Morning Show with Ed Walsh and Donna Hanover and Saturday Live with Joe Bartlett and George Meade. She is also the Life Style and Food Reporter for Saturday Home Show with Jerry Leen. On top of all that, Chef Melody still finds time to teach children to cook healthy with her "Cooking with Melody" program and to write food/restaurant stories for newspapers and magazines.

SUGGESTED WINE PAIRING

• Any of your favorite whites…
  I prefer a Pinot Grigio.

THE STORY BEHIND THE RECIPE

I have been preparing this dish on the air on WOR Radio 710 NYC for the past 15 years. Mrs. Rubschlager (her breads are used) sends the recipe to her customers and friends. This recipe is a family favorite created by three generations of Los Angeles natives: my father, Norman, Grandmother Leona Lamar, and me. Grandma Rose taught the McGinleys the spirit of Thanksgiving, spent with family and friends.

Maria's Italian Kitchen

16535 Arminta Street
Van Nuys, California 91406
818-786-4833
www.mariasitaliankitchen.com

CALIFORNIA
Restaurant
ASSOCIATION
CELEBRATING 100 YEARS OF SERVICE
1906·2006

Meatballs & Macaroni

By Chef Maria Alfano

Serves 4

INGREDIENTS

Meaty Meatballs:
2/3 lb ground chuck or sirloin
1/3 lb ground pork
3 extra-large eggs
8 oz fresh bread crumbs
8 oz Parmesan cheese
1 tsp black pepper
1 Tbs kosher salt
1/2 bunch Italian parsley,
  coarsely chopped
1/4 tsp nutmeg
1/2 medium onion, chopped fine
2 medium garlic cloves, minced

Marinara Sauce:
1/2 medium onion, finely chopped
2 oz olive oil
1/2 carrot, cleaned and finely
  chopped (optional)
2-3 garlic cloves, sliced
2 (28-oz) cans crushed Italian
  pear tomatoes
1 Tbs kosher salt, to taste
1 tsp black pepper
3-4 large fresh basil leaves, sliced
  chiffonade-roll style (optional)
1/2 bunch Italian parsley (optional)

Macaroni:
1 lb pasta (we recommend imported
  Italian spaghetti)
Salt

Garnish:
Lots of fresh grated Parmesan cheese
Fresh basil (optional)

PREPARATION INSTRUCTIONS

Meaty Meatballs: Mix meats together, then mix in all dry ingredients. Create a well in the center of meat mixture. Add eggs and mix well (wetting hands helps). We bake them at Maria's, but at home we cook them on the stove in a cast iron skillet or other heavy-bottomed pan coated with olive oil (about 2 oz). If you bake, use a preheated 325°F oven for 30 minutes or until meatballs are firm and cooked through when cut open. Remember, pork will appear pinkish when cooked.

Marinara Sauce: In an 8-quart saucepan, sauté onions in the olive oil until transparent (you may add carrots at this time) and sauté for 2 more minutes. Add sliced garlic cloves and simmer until garlic turns white. Do not burn garlic. Add crushed Italian tomatoes (have open and ready to stop garlic from overcooking). Add salt and pepper. Add meatballs to the sauce and simmer for 1-1/2 hours. Add basil and parsley.

Pasta: Bring water to a boil in large pot. Generously salt and when water is boiling rapidly, add one pound of pasta of your choice. Cook for about 8 minutes, stirring often. Drain, but do not rinse (it takes away the flavor). Put half the pasta in a big serving bowl, mix with a little sauce, then add the rest of the pasta.

Garnish: Serve with imported Parmesan cheese and a garnish of fresh basil.

Plating: Our family serves the meatballs and pasta in separate bowls, each with just enough marinara.

ABOUT THE CHEF

Maria Alfano is a native of Hoboken, New Jersey. With their five children and a suitcase full of family recipes, the Alfanos moved into Brentwood Village where Maria opened the first Maria's Italian Kitchen in 1975. Soon families were flocking to her little kitchen. The smell of fresh baked garlic bread attracted customers to the Brentwood Kitchen thirty years ago and is still bringing them to Maria's Italian Kitchens (now expanded to 10) throughout Los Angeles and Santa Barbara. Maria has been a role model and mentor to her daughter, Madelyn Alfano, who has expanded her mom's business by opening and managing the new restaurants. All food is made fresh daily. Cheese is grated fresh each day, garbanzo beans are bought from a grocer and cured by hand, Italian sausages and meatballs are homemade at Maria's every day and are never store-bought. Bread, pizza dough and pastries are baked fresh daily. Pasta is imported from Italy and served al dente, and all marinara sauce is made from scratch.

SUGGESTED WINE PAIRING

• Chianti

THE STORY BEHIND THE RECIPE

We owned a little market in Brentwood Village, where my husband and five children worked every day. In the afternoons, especially on Sunday, I would go in the back of the meat department and grind up a selection of fresh pork and chuck or sirloin; get the rest of the ingredients from the produce case and start making the meatballs and sauce (gravy).

Customers would walk through the market smelling the delicious aroma while listening to Jimmy Roselli playing over the 8-track stereo and ask me, "Maria, what are you making?" I'd say, "Sunday supper, you want some?" and that is the story of the Maria's Italian Kitchen Meatballs and Macaroni.

Masala Bowl

14311-A Newport Avenue
Tustin, California 92780
562-653-0900
www.masalabowl.com

Vegetable Samosa

By Chef Ashish Lone

Serves 10

INGREDIENTS

Dough:
1 lb refined flour
1 tsp ajwain seeds, or to taste
1/2 cup oil
3/4 cup water

Stuffing:
3 lbs boiled potatoes, drained dry and mashed
1 tsp salt
8 oz sautéed green peas
1 oz chopped cilantro
1 tsp chili powder
1 Tbs coriander powder
1 Tbs cumin powder

PREPARATION INSTRUCTIONS

Dough:
Mix all dough ingredients. Cover dough with cling film and rest it for 30 minutes. Then, ball the dough; make balls using a small ice cream scoop. Roll each dough ball into oval shape with a rolling pin, then cut in half. You should have twice as many pieces of rolled dough as balls of stuffing.

Stuffing:
Mix all ingredients for stuffing and make small balls using ice cream scoop (balls should be about 5-6 oz each).

Assembly:
Place one ball of stuffing on one piece of flattened dough, then cover with another piece of dough. Seal stuffing inside dough by pinching edges. Pinch corners to create a pyramid shape. Repeat. When dough and stuffing are used up, fry the pyramid-shaped turnovers on a low flame in enough hot vegetable oil to cover, till golden brown (about 5-6 minutes). Serve with tomato ketchup, or with mint and tamarind chutney (for a more traditional meal).

HELPFUL HINTS, VARIATIONS OR OTHER ADVICE

These samosas can be baked as well as fried. Baking is a great option for those who prefer not to eat fried food.

ABOUT THE CHEF
Ashish Lone earned a 3-year degree in Hotel Management & Catering Technology, and has 10 years of experience in the hospitality industry. Chef Ashish is trying to serve fusion food through Masala Bowl in today's modern locale, but keeping authenticity at the same time. It's fresh, fast and affordable in the unique atmosphere at Masala Bowl.

THE STORY BEHIND THE RECIPE

This is an all-time favorite food for people all over India, as well as those who know Indian food.

Mikado

12600 Riverside Drive
North Hollywood, California 91607
818-763-1963

Yuzu Citrus Tart with Fresh Berries

By Chef Alexander Kybett

Serves 2

INGREDIENTS

Tart Shell:
10 oz butter, cut into small pieces
1-1/2 cups confectioner's sugar
1/2 tsp kosher salt
1/2 tsp vanilla extract
1 Tbs yuzu or lemon zest
3-3/4 cups all purpose flour
2 eggs

Yuzu Curd:
21 oz yuzu juice, unsalted (yuzu-mitsu juice is best if available)
4 eggs
12 egg yolks
1-3/4 cups granulated sugar
1/4 tsp kosher salt
6 oz chilled butter, cut into small pieces

Garnish:
Fresh berries
Whipped cream
Mint

PREPARATION INSTRUCTIONS

Tart Shell:

Place butter and sugar in the bowl of a food processor fitted with a metal blade, and cream until soft. Add salt, vanilla and zest. Pulse food processor to combine ingredients. Add 1/3 of the flour, pulse to combine. Repeat twice until all flour is incorporated. Lightly beat eggs and add to butter and flour mixture. Pulse food processor just until dough pulls together and forms a ball. Be careful not to overwork the dough. Turn dough out onto a lightly floured work surface and form into two equal balls. Flatten dough into discs and wrap with plastic. Place in freezer for at least 45 minutes.

Remove from freezer and turn dough out on a lightly floured surface. Allow dough to thaw and roll out to 1/8-inch thick. Dock dough, place in a 9-inch tart pan and weight down with aluminum foil and beans or rice. Bake at 375°F for 20 minutes. Remove from oven. Remove foil and weight and return to oven for 10 more minutes. Remove tart shell from oven and cool to room temperature.

Yuzu Curd:

Place yuzu juice, whole eggs, egg yolks, sugar and salt in a large non-reactive bowl over simmering water. Whisk continuously over heat until ribbon stage is achieved (this takes about 15-20 minutes). When a whisk can be pulled across top of mixture and the trails of mixture do not immediately sink, the correct consistency has been achieved. Remove curd from heat and whisk butter in small additions until all butter has been used and curd has cooled slightly. Pour curd into tart shell, and place in cooler to set, about 1 hour.

Garnish:

Serve tart with fresh berries of your choice, whipped cream and mint.

ABOUT THE CHEF

Chef Alexander Kybett has worked with star chefs including Julia Child, Jacques Pepin, and Susur Lee and has won a number of culinary awards including "Best Chef in Dallas 2003" for Urban Tapas in Colleyville, TX. He has also spent time cooking in some of the best restaurants in the country and abroad including Star Canyon and Aquaknox in Dallas, the Mansion in Atlanta, and Entré Nous in St. Thomas. Alex's love of food and cooking seems to be genetic. His grandfathers were both highly acclaimed chefs – one having been personal chef to King Farouk of Egypt and the other a master chef in France. He apprenticed with both while in his teens and learned what passion for cooking was really about. Currently, Alex's French technique combined with Japanese ingredients and recipes are really taking food to the next level at Mikado Restaurant in North Hollywood, CA. His current assignment may be a bit unusual with such an illustrious resume, but the challenge of turning a sleepy restaurant, the first Japanese restaurant in the Los Angeles Valley, into a culinary destination was appealing. He is developing a contemporary, flavor-forward, Asian-fusion menu that is garnering attention in the very competitive, sushi-passionate Valley.

THE STORY BEHIND THE RECIPE

This is a "fusion" variation on a classic French "tart aux citron," this time using Asian ingredients.

The Moss Beach Distillery

140 Beach Way
Moss Beach, California 94038
650-728-5595
www.mossbeachdistillery.com

Tomato-Braised Short Ribs

By Chef Brian Barisione

Serves 4

INGREDIENTS

2-1/2 lbs short ribs
4 oz all-purpose flour
3 oz olive oil
4 oz yellow onion

4 oz carrot
1 cup tomato juice
1 cup brandy
1 cup red wine

PREPARATION INSTRUCTIONS

Coat short ribs in all-purpose flour. In pan, heat olive oil. Place flour-coated short ribs in pan. Brown short ribs on all sides. Dice yellow onions into 1/2-inch pieces. Peel carrots and dice into 1/2-inch pieces. Place diced onions and carrots in braising pan. Place short ribs on top of onions and carrots. Pour tomato juice, brandy and red wine over short ribs. Cover braising pan with parchment paper and foil. Place pan in preheated 350°F oven. Cook for 3 hours. Remove short ribs from braising liquid. Reserve braising liquid. Season braising liquid to taste with salt and black pepper.

HELPFUL HINTS, VARIATIONS OR OTHER ADVICE

You can substitute lamb shank or cross rib roast to make a pot roast.

ABOUT THE CHEF

Brian Barisione started his love for cooking as a child by helping his grandmother in the kitchen. By age 16, Brian was working as a cook or dishwasher in restaurants around the San Francisco Bay Area. After doing this for several years, he enrolled in The California Culinary Academy. After graduation, Brian went to work for several hotels and worked in corporate catering in the San Francisco Bay Area. During this time he cooked for numerous sports teams, political figures, foreign dignitaries and many of Silicon Valley's high powered executives. Brian came to The Moss Beach Distillery in late 2003. He brought many influences and strives to use the best in organic produce, fresh seafood and natural meat.

SUGGESTED WINE PAIRING

• 2004 Bonny Doon Cardinal Zin, Santa Cruz

THE STORY BEHIND THE RECIPE

The inspiration comes from a lamb dish my grandmother used to make. When I was a child, my grandmother would make a similar dish using lamb shank every Easter. It is my favorite dish on our menu.

New Leaf Restaurant & Bar
@ Hilton San Diego Gaslamp Quarter

401 K Street
San Diego, California 92101
619-702-8271
www.sandiegogaslampquarter.hilton.com

Grilled NY Strip with Organic Swiss Chard, Truffle Tater Tots and Bloody Mary Sauce

By Chef Billy Deaver, Jr.

Serves 1

INGREDIENTS

Strip Steak:
1 12-oz NY strip steak
2 tsp fresh ground coffee or espresso
Salt and pepper

Swiss Chard:
2 leaves organic swiss chard, chopped
1/4 cup olive oil (do not use extra virgin, it will burn and emit a bitter flavor in your food)
3 cloves garlic
1/4 cup white wine

Potatoes:
1 Yukon Gold potato
1 baking potato
2 cloves garlic, chopped
1 sprig rosemary
1 fresh bay leaf
1 cup potato starch
1 oz chives, chopped
1 whole egg
1 oz truffle oil

Bloody Mary Sauce:
2 cups Bloody Mary mix
4 cups veal stock
1 oz butter, unsalted (Plugra preferred)
Salt and pepper

PREPARATION INSTRUCTIONS

Steak: Start off by sprinkling the coffee liberally on both sides of the steak with salt and pepper. Let sit for about 30 minutes. Grill the steak for about 3-4 minutes on each side, then finish in a oven pre-heated to 350°F for another 5 minutes (medium rare).

Swiss Chard: While you are waiting, chop the swiss chard and dunk it into a bowl of cold water to remove all dirt. Place on a paper towel to absorb all excess water. On a medium-high setting, heat some olive oil in a sauté pan. Once hot, toss in the garlic and the swiss chard. Add white wine and remove from heat.

Potatoes: Rinse potatoes and place in a pot with garlic, rosemary and bay leaf. Boil until soft. Remove and, while hot, take off the skin of the potatoes and grate them on a cheese grater. Mix with the potato starch, chives, egg, truffle oil and salt and pepper. Chill. Once chilled place in a piping bag and pipe onto sheet pan in long lines, cut to desired length and freeze until later. Before plate-up remove the tater tots from the freezer and place in the pre-heated oven for 12-15 minutes or deep fry them at 330°F for 4-6 minutes or until golden brown.

(cont'd)

ABOUT THE CHEF

Chef Billy Deaver, Jr. is a second-generation chef who began his career at an early age working on his family's farm cultivating table vegetables and tending to some of the animals which they raised and butchered. It was not until years later that he found himself enrolled in classes and working for Certified Master Chef Detlev Kreiner that he knew he had found his career and passion. After working with Chef Detlev, Chef Billy started his way up north to Hamilton Township, NJ to work with Eric Martin at Rats and later on to New York City to have the brilliant opportunity to spend time with Daniel Bollud at Daniel's and Pino Luongo at Le Madri. Since, he has traveled the country working in Philadelphia, Atlanta, Myrtle Beach, Lake Tahoe and has since found his new resting place, San Diego, leading the kitchen of Molly's which he brought to the level of a four-diamond restaurant in both 2004 and 2005. Chef Billy is currently at the helm of the kitchen in the beautiful Hilton San Diego Gaslamp Quarter where his style of New American cuisine marks his new home.

PREPARATION INSTRUCTIONS
(cont'd)

Bloody Mary Sauce: Place Bloody Mary mix in a pan and reduce by half. Add veal stock and reduce by half. Check seasonings. Add salt and pepper, if needed. One minute prior to plate-up, whisk in butter.

Plating: Place the chard on the plate, off-center. Slice steak five or six times and place on top of chard. On the opposite side of the plate stack the tater tots. Spoon the Bloody Mary sauce down the middle.

SUGGESTED WINE PAIRING

• 2003 Justin Isoseles

THE STORY BEHIND THE RECIPE

This dish is a spin on the classic meat and potatoes which will appeal to both the traditionalist and the adventurous. This is a menu item I like to push, asking diners to order something that they would not usually order. I tell them if they don't like it I will buy it for them and, so far, I have not had to buy any dinners.

Nine Thirty Restaurant
@ The W Hotel Los Angeles

930 Hilgard Avenue
Los Angeles, California 90024
310-208-8765
www.ninethirtyw.com

Curry Duck Burger

By Chef Jack Yoss

Serves 10

INGREDIENTS

Burgers:
2 lbs ground duck meat
1/2 bunch mint
1/2 bunch cilantro
1/2 bunch Thai basil
1 garlic clove
1 small piece ginger
2-3 Tbs fish sauce
1/2 Tbs red curry paste (maeploy)

Aioli:
1 egg yolk
1/4 tsp curry powder
1/2 lime, juiced
1/4 tsp tumeric powder
1 cup grapeseed oil
1/2 tsp fish sauce
Salt and pepper

Foccacia, preferably roasted onion

Celery root:
1 small celery root
1 green apple
2 Tbs crème fraiche
1/2 lime, juiced
Salt and pepper

Garnish:
1 small jar orange marmalade

PREPARATION INSTRUCTIONS

Burgers:

In a food processor, blend mint, cilantro, thai basil, garlic, ginger and curry paste. Mix duck with half the purée, reserve the remains, then fold in approximately 2-3 Tbs of fish sauce. Form into 2 oz patties.

Aioli:

In blender place egg yolk, 1/2 of the reserved purée, curry powder, lime juice and tumeric. Turn on medium setting, slowly adding the oil. Add 1/2 teaspoon fish sauce. Add more purée if desired, salt and pepper to taste.

Celery root:

Peel celery root, then julienne. Julienne apple, but do not peel. Place them in a mixing bowl and add crème fraiche, lime juice and salt and pepper, to taste.

To assemble:

Cut foccacia into two inch squares, cut in half like a bun. Brown duck patties in medium-high skillet about two to three minutes on each side until cooked about medium. Toast foccacia in oven. Spread curry aioli on foccacia. Place duck on bread and top with small dollop of orange marmalade. Top with small amount of celery root mix.

HELPFUL HINTS, VARIATIONS OR OTHER ADVICE

This recipe is kid-friendly. Ground beef, veal, turkey or pork can be substituted for duck.

ABOUT THE CHEF

Jack Yoss' love for cooking began at the young age of ten while preparing family meals for his younger siblings. His professional career began at age 16, when Yoss quickly ascended the ranks in a Las Vegas hotel restaurant, then worked as a line cook at Nero's, an upscale American steakhouse in the chic Caesar's Palace. The sophisticated ingredients and upscale menu items would later become a signature of Yoss' style. Ever ambitious, Yoss set his eyes on Wolfgang Puck's exclusive Chinois Restaurant. His ambition, persistence and extraordinary talents helped secure him the position of Saucier at Chinois, where he worked for a year creating deliciously decadent sauces for Chinois' succulent cuisine. In 1999, Yoss moved to what he considered the source of upscale culinary cuisine, San Francisco, to become Pantry Cook at the highly regarded Postrio Restaurant. Securing the role of Sous Chef and eventually Chef de Cuisine, Yoss gained local notoriety in a high-profile culinary market. Yoss garnered a strong reputation among his peers as well, including Chef Jacques Pepin, who last year nominated Yoss for *Food & Wine's* "Best New Chefs in America" competition. Each night, Chef Yoss can be seen greeting and chatting with diners at NineThirty Restaurant.

SUGGESTED WINE PAIRING

- 2001 Louis Latour Pinot Noir

THE STORY BEHIND THE RECIPE

Chef Yoss' Curry Duck Burgers were created as a modern take on three classic culinary dishes: Curry Duck, Duck a la Orange and Duck with Apples and Celery Root. This dish was inspired by Chef's favorite Thai spices and classic French techniques.

Noé Restaurant

251 South Olive Street, 3rd Floor
Los Angeles, California 90012
213-356-4100
www.noerestaurant.com

Potato and Almond Milk Soup with California Raisins and Pumpkin Seeds

By Chef Robert Gadsby

Serves 4

INGREDIENTS

Soup:

1/2 cup extra virgin olive oil
1 medium onion, chopped
3 Tbs salt (or more, as needed for taste)
1 lb Yukon Gold or other potatoes, peeled and chopped
1 cup whole milk
1-1/2 Tbs almond oil (available at specialty stores)
Ground white pepper, salt and sugar to taste
1 cup (6 oz) California raisins (dark and golden, mixed)
4 oz toasted pumpkin seeds
2 Tbs extra virgin olive oil
Almond oil
Chopped chives

Almond Whipped Cream:

1 cup heavy cream
1-1/2 Tbs almond oil (available at specialty stores)
Salt and sugar, to taste

PREPARATION INSTRUCTIONS

Whipped Cream:

Season the cream with a pinch of salt and sugar. Whip with an electric beater. When the cream is almost stiff enough, add the almond oil; beat for 10-25 seconds more. Set aside and refrigerate until needed.

Soup:

In a large saute pan or sauce pan over medium heat, saute onion in 1/2 cup olive oil, season with salt and stir to coat. Add the chopped potatoes and continue stirring until potatoes are heated through. Add the milk to cover (about 1/2-inch deep), add 1-1/2 Tbs almond oil, and simmer until potatoes are completely tender. Drain, reserving the cooking liquid, and puree potatoes in a blender, adding enough of the reserved liquid to form a silky smooth potato soup. Taste and correct the seasoning with salt, sugar and white pepper.

Plating:

Reheat soup. Divide the raisins and the pumpkin seeds among 4 soup bowls and drizzle with 1/2 Tbs olive oil per bowl. Pour soup into bowls, placing a dollop of almond whipped cream near the rim of each bowl and drizzling a little almond oil on the cream. Sprinkle with soup with chopped chives and serve.

HELPFUL HINTS, VARIATIONS OR OTHER ADVICE

Soup can be served with Golden Thompson grapes, California raisins and onion marmalade.

ABOUT THE CHEF

Leaving his hometown of Bedford, England, Gadsby trained more than 30 years ago at Westminster Culinary Academy in London. Gadsby apprenticed with the legendary Alain Chapel, Joel Robuchon and Alain Ducasse and furthered his culinary education in Asia before moving to the United States in 1985. With the opening of the eponymous GADSBYS in 1995, Chef Gadsby truly came into his own. From the plates on the table to the logo, everything was handpicked or designed by the Gadsby family. Now with Noé Restaurant & Bar at the Omni Los Angeles Hotel, Gadsby redefines the notion of hotel dining. His progressive American cuisine has garnered critical accolades including "Best of the Year" Issue – *Bon Appétit*, Top Ten New Restaurants – *Los Angeles* Magazine, and "★★ 1/2 stars" – *Los Angeles Times*.

Gadsby and Omni Hotels expanded the concept to Houston in 2004, where in its first year, the restaurant was awarded "Best New Restaurant" by the *Houston Press* and *My Table* magazine; "Best of the Best" by *Robb Report* and the *Houston Chronicle*; and "Chef of the Year" honors from *My Table*. Gadsby and Omni Hotels opened 676 Restaurant & Bar, a New American brasserie in the Omni Chicago Hotel, in October 2005.

THE STORY BEHIND THE RECIPE

The combination of flavors is quite sophisticated, and the soup is a hit whenever served.

NutriFit LLC

11692 Gateway Boulevard
Los Angeles, California 90064
310-473-1989
www.nutrifitonline.com

CALIFORNIA
Restaurant
ASSOCIATION
CELEBRATING 100 YEARS OF SERVICE
1906-2006

Quinoa Super Salad

By Chef Jacqueline Keller

Serves 8

INGREDIENTS

Salad:
5 cups quinoa, cooked according to package instructions
1 cup Italian green beans
1 cup carrots, diced
1/2 cup Italian parsley, finely chopped
1/4 cup black olives, sliced
1/2 cup sunflower seed kernels

Dressing:
1 Tbs extra virgin olive oil
1/4 cup fresh lemon juice
1/4 cup reduced sodium tamari

Garnish:
1 cup fresh tomatoes, seeded and chopped

PREPARATION INSTRUCTIONS

Salad:
Steam green beans until tender but still crisp, or, if using frozen, defrost and drain. Cook quinoa and let cool. Add carrots, parsley, olives, green beans and seeds to quinoa. Mix thoroughly.

Dressing:
Combine ingedients, pour over quinoa and toss well.

Plating:
Garnish with tomatoes.

HELPFUL HINTS, VARIATIONS OR OTHER ADVICE

To remove the bitter saponin coating that is a part of this grain, rinse it well in cold water before cooking. Cook 1 cup of quinoa in 2 cups of liquid. For added flavor, cook the quinoa in low-fat, reduced-sodium chicken or vegetable broth. May be enjoyed cold, warm or at room temperature.

THE STORY BEHIND THE RECIPE

I designed this recipe while writing *Body After Baby* after learning about the amazing nutritional value of quinoa, a super grain. The dish provides the ingredients necessary for a complete vegetarian protein, and is rich in other nutrients. Quinoa is just as versatile as rice or couscous. I thought it would be a good idea to pair it with other "super foods," like tomatoes, sunflower seeds, olives and olive oil.

ABOUT THE CHEF

Jacqueline Keller, a healthy-lifestyle coach, nutrition educator and culinary expert, is the Founding Director of NutriFit, LLC, author of *Body After Baby: The Simple 30 Day Plan to Lose Your Baby Weight* (Avery/Penguin Group; May 2006), and *Cooking, Eating & Living Well*, a cookbook and guide to nutrition-related lifestyle change. In 1987, Jackie and her partner, husband Phil Yaney, formed NutriFit as a nutritional services and health education company. NutriFit boasts a healthy food delivery service that offers healthful meals designed to accommodate an individual's health and lifestyle needs. Their goal is to promote long-term health by providing full-service nutritional support, including meals, dietary counseling and health-related products. NutriFit has provided nutritional services to celebrities such as Uma Thurman, Angelina Jolie, Charlize Theron, Will Ferrell, Jack Black, Penelope Cruz, Susan Sarandon, Val Kilmer, Tia Carrere, Billy Bob Thornton, Jake Gyllenhaal, Topher Grace, Lucy Liu and fitness guru Kathy Smith, as well as conducting education classes for more than 1,000 companies nationwide.

On the Waterfront Cafe

205 Ocean Front Walk
Venice, California 90291
310-392-0322
www.waterfrontcafe.com

Linguine Fisherman

By Chef Stefan Bachofner

Serves 6

INGREDIENTS

1 lb linguine or spaghetti
20 black tiger shrimp
20 medium scallops
Juice from 1/2 lemon
Salt and pepper

Sauce:
1/2 onion
1 clove garlic
1 tomato
1 Tbs butter or olive oil

1-2 Tbs curry (depending on how hot you like the sauce)
1 oz white wine
3 oz cream
Parsley

PREPARATION INSTRUCTIONS

Pasta:

Set up a pot with water, salt and oil to cook your pasta.

Shrimp & Scallops:

Peel tiger shrimp and cut in half. Marinate the scallops and the shrimp with lemon juice, salt and pepper. Let stand.

Sauce:

Dice the onion, garlic and tomato. Preheat a frying pan and sauté onions and garlic in butter or olive oil, adding in scallops and shrimp. Stir in tomatoes. Sprinkle curry powder over ingredients in the pan and sauté lightly. When curry has mixed up well with other ingredients add white wine. Let wine reduce almost completely. Add cream and reduce to a sauce consistency. Meanwhile cut parsley into thin flakes.

Plating:

Make a bed of linguine on preheated plates. Equally distribute shrimp and scallops on the linguine beds. Pour curry sauce on linguine and garnish with the parsley flakes.

HELPFUL HINTS, VARIATIONS OR OTHER ADVICE

When preparing larger quantities it is better to take the scallops and shrimp out of the pan after they have been sautéed. This way they won't overcook in the process of reducing the white wine and the cream.

ABOUT THE CHEF

Stefan Bachofner was born in 1967 in Zurich, Switzerland. He graduated from the Hotel Management School in Thun, Switzerland and has been working as a chef since 1984. Stefan has worked at the high-class restaurant 18 Gault Millaut Point, in Zurich, and in food and beverage management and purchase for a large shopping mall with seven restaurants and two food supermarkets in Moscow, Russia. Stefan has owned On the Waterfront Cafe since 1994.

SUGGESTED WINE PAIRING

- J. Lohr Chardonnay, Paso Robles
- Ecco Domani Pinot Grigio

THE STORY BEHIND THE RECIPE

This recipe is a favorite of our clientele at our highly frequented restaurant, which is right on the boardwalk in Venice. It had been on the menu here since 1986, created by the former French chef Jean Paul.

P6 Restaurant & Lounge

2809 Agoura Road
Westlake Village, California 91362
805-778-0123/2
www.p6lounge.com

Phyllo-Wrapped Jumbo Sea Scallops with Smoked Salmon, Vodka Chive Crème Fraîche and Osetra Caviar

By Chef Robert Lia

Serves 6

INGREDIENTS

6 (U-10) jumbo sea scallops seared rare and chilled
2 Tbs melted butter
Phyllo dough
6 oz smoked salmon
Vodka crème fraîche (recipe follows)
1 oz osetra caviar

Vodka Crème Fraîche:
1 cup vodka
3 Tbs shallots, chopped
2 cups cream
1/2 cup sour cream
Pinch of salt
Pinch of sugar

PREPARATION INSTRUCTIONS

Vodka Crème Fraîche:

In a medium saucepan, bring vodka and shallots to a simmer (carefully, as this is very flammable). Let reduce by half. Add cream and sour cream. Return to a simmer. Blend, strain and return to a simmer. Reduce by half. Season to taste with salt and sugar. Reserve warm.

Scallops:

Slice scallops into three slices each. Butter one sheet of phyllo and carefully place another sheet atop. Repeat until 4 phyllo sheets are used. Cut phyllo into six equal squares. Place one slice of scallop in the center of each phyllo square. Top scallop with a small slice of smoked salmon, same size as scallop. Repeat until all scallops are used. Fold edges of phyllo towards center of scallop, as to envelope scallop and smoked salmon napoleon. (Note: Wrap phyllo tightly around napoleon). Bake at 375°F for 10 minutes or until crispy and light brown.

Plating:

Julienne remainder of smoked salmon. Divide equally among 6 plates, in the center. Top with osetra caviar. Slice phyllo-scallop napoleon in half and place aside smoked salmon. Spoon Vodka Crème Fraîche sauce around, garnish with chives.

HELPFUL HINTS, VARIATIONS OR OTHER ADVICE

Use ready-to-go phyllo dough. It cuts down the prep time and makes a more consistent product.

ABOUT THE CHEF

Executive Chef Robert Lia shaped dining trends at some of Los Angeles' most celebrated restaurants before being lured to P6 Restaurant & Lounge, not far from where he grew up in the San Fernando Valley. During high school, he landed a job on the line at Brio, a California cuisine restaurant where he was mentored by acclaimed L.A. chef André Guerrero and eventually advanced to Sous Chef.

After studying at Pierce College, Lia enlisted in the Navy, where he was stationed in Italy for five years, giving him an opportunity to eat and drink his way through Europe, refining his palate and occasionally cooking. After re-entering civilian life in 1996, Lia joined 72 Market Street, the legendary Venice restaurant known for its impromptu performances by celebrity co-owner Dudley Moore while guests enjoyed classic American fare. During his two-year tenure as Chef de Cuisine, he co-authored the lushly photographed cookbook, 72 Market Street Dishes It Out! with his colleague and mentor, Roland Gilbert. In 1997, Lia became a partner in Bel-Air Bar & Grill, where as Executive Chef he cooked a contemporary California cuisine that prepared him well for his subsequent assignment in 1999, as Executive Chef at Geoffrey's, the renowned Malibu restaurant sitting atop a bluff overlooking the Pacific. In 2003, he transitioned from an almost exclusively al fresco restaurant to one of the most lavishly decorated dining rooms in Los Angeles, the Lalique glass-clad Cicada in the Art Deco landmark Oviatt Building. As Executive Chef at Cicada, he created a modern Italian menu that received enthusiastic reviews from the culinary press.

In 2005, Lia served as Executive Chef at the Sheraton Delfina Hotel in Santa Monica until the partners of 2K5 Details, Inc. (the restaurant group that owns and operates P6 and Chapter 8) immediately called on Lia, whose balance of classic technique and contemporary innovation were ideal for positioning P6 as the premier fine dining venue in the Conejo Valley.

SUGGESTED WINE PAIRING

• Ayala Brut Champagne, NV or 2003 Chassagne Montrachet Blanchot-Dessus

THE STORY BEHIND THE RECIPE

This is a signature dish of P6 Restaurant & Lounge.

Pasta Pomodoro

Various in Northern California -
Bay Area and Sacramento
San Francisco, California 94103
415-241-5222
www.pastapomodoro.com

CALIFORNIA
Restaurant
ASSOCIATION
CELEBRATING 100 YEARS OF SERVICE
1906-2006

pomodoro™

Polenta Farcita

By Chef Adriano Paganini

Serves 3-5

INGREDIENTS

Polenta:
1 cup corn meal (polenta)
1 qt water
1 Tbs salt
2 oz butter

Filling:
6 oz fontina cheese, sliced
1/2 cup Parmesan cheese, grated
6 oz steamed spinach

Topping:
Butter
Fresh sage leaves

PREPARATION INSTRUCTIONS

Polenta:
Place water in a saucepot and bring to boil. Add salt. Add corn meal, stirring constantly with a whisk to avoid lumps. Cook for 35 minutes over low flame. Add butter and mix well.

Filling:
Lay some plastic wrap on the bottom of a cookie sheet. Spread polenta evenly on bottom of pan so that it is 1/2-inch thick. Next, spread cheeses and spinach evenly on polenta and roll to a cylinder (log) shape. Let cool, then cut roll in slices. Arrange on a plate and bake for 5 minutes at 375°F. Top with browned butter and sage.

Topping:
Melt some butter in a pan over medium heat. Once the butter is melted, add the fresh sage leaves. Cook until the butter has turned brown and the sage leaves are crispy.

ABOUT THE CHEF

Adriano Paganini grew up as the son of a family of tailors in a small village outside of Milan. Even as a small child, Adriano preferred eating to sewing. Inspired by his mother's simple style of cooking with the freshest ingredients, Adriano's passion for food grew. As a young man, he studied culinary arts in Varese and was later selected to apprentice with the world-famous Paul Bocuse in France and Gualtiero Marchesi, a three Michelin star in Italy, before moving to London. A gifted five-star chef, Adriano became Executive Chef at the main dining restaurant at London's Hyde Park Hotel at the tender age of 24, where he cooked for such famous guests as the Queen of England, the President of Italy, U.S. President Ronald Reagan and Luciano Pavarotti. Upon arriving in America, Adriano chose to set up Pasta Pomodoro restaurants - contemporary Italian cuisine and style at extremely affordable prices. Now boasting 46 restaurants to his name, Adriano's vision was to continuously develop his minimalist approach and distance his concept from the more traditional trattoria restaurants that most people associate with Italian food.

SUGGESTED WINE PAIRING

- 2004 St. Francis Chardonnay

THE STORY BEHIND THE RECIPE

It's an old recipe that not only is renowned as a comfort dish but brings back memories of growing up in Italy. It's a staple food and a typical dish of Italy.

Pleasanton Hotel

855 Main Street
Pleasanton, California 94566
925-846-8106
www.pleasantonhotel.com

CALIFORNIA
Restaurant
ASSOCIATION
CELEBRATING 100 YEARS OF SERVICE
1906-2006

....

Dungeness Crab and Fennel Spring Rolls with Black Bean Dragon Sauce

By Chef Neil Marquis

Serves 10

INGREDIENTS

Spring Rolls:
1/2 lb Dungeness crab meat
1/2 head fennel, julienned
1 tsp sugar
1 Tbs butter
1/2 lb cream cheese, room temperature
1 Tbs ginger, minced
1/2 Tbs garlic, minced
1/4 cup cilantro, chopped
1/4 tsp chopped mint
1 Tbs rayu (spicy sesame oil)
1 tsp sachimi

Springroll wrappers
Cornstarch
Water

Black Bean Dragon Sauce:
1/4 pkg Chinese fermented black beans
4 Tbs sweet Thai chili sauce
1 small batch Dragon Base (recipe below)

Dragon Base:
1/4 cup frozen orange juice, from concentrate

1/2 cup white wine vinegar
1/2 cup sugar
3 kaffir lime leaves
3 oz chopped lemongrass
3 oz chopped ginger with skin
Cornstarch slurry to thicken

Cilantro Oil:
3/4 cup chopped cilantro
1/4 cup vegetable oil

Soy Mustard:
1/2 cup Dijon mustard
2 Tbs soy sauce

PREPARATION INSTRUCTIONS

Spring Rolls: Caramelize fennel and sugar in butter. Put cream cheese, ginger, garlic, cilantro and mint in a food processor, pulse until all ingredients are incorporated. Add rayu and sachimi. Transfer cream cheese mix to a medium mixing bowl and add crab meat and fennel. Mix well and chill. Place 3 oz of filling onto each spring roll wrap and roll like a spring roll, using water to seal. Dredge in cornstarch to prevent the rolls from sticking together. Fry the rolls in hot oil and serve.

Dragon Base: Combine all ingredients except cornstarch in heavy-bottom stainless steel pot and bring to a boil. Add cornstarch slurry and reduce heat to a simmer for 30 minutes. Strain through fine sieve.

Dragon Sauce: Rinse beans in cold water to remove all salt. Add remaining ingredients to heavy bottom stainless steel pot and bring to a boil. Reduce heat and simmer for 10 minutes. Add black beans and keep sauce warm for serving.

Cilantro Oil: Put oil and cilantro in blender and purée on high until all cilantro is puréed. Put mixture in heavy bottom pot and bring to a boil. Reduce heat and simmer for 15 mins. Strain oil through a coffee filter, put in squeeze bottle and refrigerate unused portion.

Soy Mustard: Mix mustard and soy, place in squeeze bottle for service.

ABOUT THE CHEF
Chef Neil Marquis has worked in the food industry for 26 years. Some of his career highlights include working for Bill Graham Presents doing backstage and movie location catering, working in France and on the top of the mountain in Vail, Colorado.

HELPFUL HINTS, VARIATIONS OR OTHER ADVICE
You can also add avocado to this dish.

SUGGESTED WINE PAIRING
• 2005 Grgich Chardonnay

THE STORY BEHIND THE RECIPE
This recipe won Spengers 5th Annual Crabby Chef Competition, a 20-minute Iron Chef-style competition featuring twenty-two of the top San Francisco Bay area chefs.

Pomodoro Cucina Italiana

Various in Southern California -
Los Angeles, Orange County, San Fernando Valley
c/o San Francisco, California 94103
415-241-5222
www.pastapomodoro.com

CALIFORNIA
Restaurant
ASSOCIATION
CELEBRATING 100 YEARS OF SERVICE
1906-2006

Gamberi

By Chef Edmondo Sarti

Serves 2-4

INGREDIENTS

2 Tbs butter
2 Tbs garlic, chopped
10 fresh shrimp
1 tsp chili flakes
1 Tbs fresh parsley, chopped

Salt and fresh pepper, to taste
1/3 cup white wine
1 Tbs lemon juice
1/3 cup tomato sauce

PREPARATION INSTRUCTIONS

Melt butter in a pan. Add garlic and lightly sauté. Add shrimp and sauté on both sides. Add chili, parsley, salt and pepper. Deglaze pan with wine and lemon juice and reduce by half. Add tomato sauce and bring to a boil, being careful not to overcook the shrimp. Serve with grilled rustic bread brushed with garlic.

ABOUT THE CHEF

Edmondo Sarti joined Pasta Pomodoro in May 2002. Edmondo's career began at the age of 13 working in his uncle's restaurant making pizzas in the small Italian town of Portomaggiore. Edmondo attended culinary school in Cervia, Italy prior to being drafted into the military where he became the chef at the Officer's Restaurant. After the service, he moved to England where he accepted a Sous Chef position at the Hyde Park Hotel cooking for many dignitaries including the Queen and former Prime Minister Margaret Thatcher. Edmondo's first position in the U.S. was in Los Angeles, CA working with Piero Selvaggio, owner of Valentino Restaurant. He then moved on to Il Fornaio where he worked in Costa Mesa, Beverly Hills, Corte Madera and San Francisco. As Executive Chef of Pomodoro, Edmondo quickly established the launch of the Southern California Pomodoro restaurants which are now extremely popular and a fixture in the contemporary Italian dining scene.

SUGGESTED WINE PAIRING

- 2004 Edna Valley Sauvignon Blanc

THE STORY BEHIND THE RECIPE

We tested this dish in our Laguna Beach restaurant before introducing it to all our restaurants. It's a traditional dish, but we add lobster stock, which is expensive, but adds our signature flavor to the dish.

Pure Joy Catering, Inc.

710 East Haley Street
Santa Barbara, California 93103
805-963-5766
www.purejoycatering.com

Pure Joy Catering
Fabulous Full Service Events

Pollo con Higos Borachos (Tender Bronzed Chicken Doused with Saucy Drunken Figs)

By Chef Lynette La Mere

Serves 4

INGREDIENTS

Figs:
3/4 cup sugar
3/4 cup water
1/3 cup red wine vinegar
1 slice of lemon
1 cinnamon stick
1 lb fresh black mission figs

3/4 cup pinot noir
Zest of 1/2 lemon

Chicken:
4 boneless, skinless chicken breasts
(or 4 to 6 pieces of bone-in chicken)
Salt and pepper, to taste
3 slices of bacon, cut up

1 Tbs olive oil
3 Tbs chicken stock
1 Tbs lemon juice

PREPARATION INSTRUCTIONS

Figs: In a medium-sized heavy-bottom sauce pan bring to a boil sugar, water, vinegar, lemon slice and cinnamon stick. Simmer 5 minutes. Add the whole figs, return to a boil and simmer over medium-low heat 10 minutes more, swirling them around occasionally. Remove from heat and cover or let sit out several hours or overnight. 45 minutes before dinner will be served, transfer figs to a small bowl reserving fig soaking liquid. Discard cinnamon stick and lemon slice. Pour wine and lemon zest over figs in small bowl. Let sit while preparing chicken.

Chicken: Season chicken well with salt and pepper. In a large cast iron or heavy skillet slowly heat bacon pieces until they begin to turn golden and give off their oil. Remove bacon and add olive oil to bacon oil already in the pan. Sauté chicken over high heat until golden on all sides, approximately 7 minutes on each side. Remove chicken from pan and add wine the figs have been soaking in. Leave heat high and reduce sauce 5 minutes. Add original reserved fig stewing liquid and reduce over high heat an additional 3 to 4 minutes. Add chicken stock and lemon juice to the pan. Return chicken with any accumulated juices, the figs and bacon pieces as well if you want. (The bacon can also be crumbled on top later or discarded.) Simmer 5 to 10 minutes more turning chicken over halfway through. Turn off heat and allow to rest and thicken a few moments.

Plating: Top each breast with a quarter of sauce and figs.

HELPFUL HINTS, VARIATIONS OR OTHER ADVICE

You can prepare the figs several hours or a day in advance. If you are using boneless chicken breasts you only need to initially brown them 3 minutes per side.

ABOUT THE CHEF

Lynette La Mere is the Executive Chef of a Santa Barbara-based special-event catering company who began her life in the culinary arts at her grandfather's side. Today we share his love of all things edible, his endless curiosity and pride in creating and serving spectacular special event meals to an average of 18,000 wedding guests a year.

SUGGESTED WINE PAIRING

• 2003 Carlson Pinot Noir

THE STORY BEHIND THE RECIPE

I cannot discuss figs without a nod to my beloved grandfather, whose contagious passion for life and food was unparalleled. While many of those around us pooh-poohed the humble little fruits, he raved of their value and shared it with me. In his "Shangri-La" home, he ceremonially planted a fig tree for me. Every Fall I had one of the truest joys life offers, that of picking ripe fruit from a spectacular tree and enjoying its pleasures. To this day, I cannot keep my eyes open while eating a sun-ripened fig.

Rattlesnake at Spotlight 29 Casino

46-200 Harrison Place
Coachella, California 92236
760-863-2404
www.spotlight29.com

Spice-Crusted Pineapple Steak with Ginger Ice Cream

By Chef Jimmy Schmidt

Serves 4

INGREDIENTS

Pineapple Steaks:
1 large pineapple
1 Tbs whole black tellicherry peppercorns
1 tsp white peppercorns
1 tsp whole allspice
2 tsp coarse sea salt
Pinch red chili flakes
1 tsp granulated onion

1 tsp granulated garlic
1 tsp dried orange rind
2 Tbs unsalted butter
1 Tbs minced fresh ginger
4 Tbs palm or turbinado sugar
1 cup sake
1 vanilla bean, cut lengthwise, seeds scraped

Ginger White Chocolate Ice Cream:
4 cups sake
1/2 cup fine diced preserved ginger
12 ounces half and half
1/2 cup turbinado sugar
10 pasteurized egg yolks
8 ounces white chocolate
1 Tbs pure vanilla extract
Pinch salt

PREPARATION INSTRUCTIONS

Pineapple Steaks:

To cut pineapple steaks, first trim pineapple of its outer skin and eyes. Then cut the pineapple in four even sections from the top to the base of about 4 inches long. On a cutting board or butcher block combine black and white peppercorns with allspice. With the edge of a heavy skillet coarsely crush the spices. Transfer to a fine sieve to sift off fine spice powder (save as a pepper blend for other dishes). Transfer coarse peppercorns to a small bowl and mix in coarse sea salt, chile flakes, onion, garlic and orange rind. Firmly press surface of pineapple steaks into peppercorn mix to affix to the surface. In a large, heavy, non-stick skillet heat butter over medium high heat. Add ginger, cooking until tender (about 2 minutes). Add pineapple, cooking until it begins to soften slightly (about 3 minutes). Add sugar, cooking until well caramelized and very tender (about 8 minutes). Add sake and vanilla seeds, cooking until liquids are reduced to make a tight syrup. Remove from heat. Place pineapple steaks, flat side up, in the center of serving plate.

(cont'd)

ABOUT THE CHEF

Jimmy Schmidt, a native Midwesterner, opened The Rattlesnake Club in June of 1988 and, following its success, opened the Rattlesnake at the Spotlight 29 Casino in Palm Springs, California in 2002. Over the years, many prestigious awards have been bestowed upon Schmidt and the Rattlesnake Club including the Ivy Award, the James Beard Foundation's "Best Chef of the Midwest," *Gourmet's* "America's Top Tables" and "America's Best Restaurants," *Wine Spectator's* "Award Winning Wine Lists," the DiRoNA Award and the American Academy of Hospitality Sciences' "Star Diamond Award." Schmidt is the Director of Sports Nutrition for GM/Corvette Racing and coordinates catering services for the "24 Hours of LeMans" endurance race in LeMans, France. He is also working on many nutritional product-development projects with Functional Foods Co. Schmidt has authored and co-authored several cookbooks including *Cooking for all Seasons* (MacMillan, 1991), *Jimmy Schmidt's Cooking Class* (Detroit Free Press, 1994) and *Heart Healthy Cooking for all Seasons* released in 1996. Schmidt writes a weekly column for the *Detroit News/Gannett Wire Services* appearing in 200 newspapers across the country. He actively serves on the Board of Overseers of Chefs Collaborative and is a member of the Young President's Organization (YPO), successfully completing several YPO Executive Training Seminars at Harvard Business School. Schmidt is also one of the founding chefs of the culinary charity Share Our Strength. Schmidt and the Rattlesnake Club are annual participants in the American Chefs' Tribute to James Beard benefiting City Meals-on-Wheels in New York City and Wolfgang Puck's American Wine & Food Festival benefiting Meals-on-Wheels in Los Angeles. While studying electrical engineering at the University of Illinois, Schmidt traveled to France to obtain foreign language credits toward his degree. He stayed to pursue a culinary career and received the French Classic and Provincial Culinary Arts diploma from Luberon College, Avignon, France, and the French Institute Technique du Vin diploma from Maison du Vin in Avignon in 1974. In 1976, he received his Professional Chef's diploma Magna Cum Laude, graduating First in Class, from Modern Gourmet, Inc., Newton Centre, Massachusetts, under the direction of Madeleine Kamman. After serving as Senior Chef at Chez La Mere Madeleine, New Centre, MA, he moved to Detroit in 1977 to become Executive Chef and Executive General Manager of the London Chop House.

PREPARATION INSTRUCTIONS
(cont'd)

Ginger White Chocolate Ice Cream:

In a small saucepan, combine sake with ginger over medium heat, cooking until reduced to 3/4 cup. Add half and half and bring to a scald. Remove from heat. In a medium saucepan combine sugar and yolks. Whisk in warm cream mixture. Place on medium heat, cooking while constantly stirring until thickened to coat the back of a spoon. Immediately pour over white chocolate in a large bowl, stirring to dissolve chocolate and stop the cooking. Stir in vanilla and salt. Stir until very smooth. Process in an ice cream maker, according to the manufacturer's instructions, until just about solid. Pour and smooth into a plastic-wrap-lined, small, square metal baking pan so that the ice cream makes a depth of 2 inches. Cover well and freeze until solid overnight.

Plating:

Using a round pastry cutter, cut and remove a piece of ice cream to match the center of the pineapple. Drizzle the caramelized pan sauce over the ice cream and around the plate.

HELPFUL HINTS, VARIATIONS OR OTHER ADVICE

The pineapple steak plays a sweet and savory twist on the palate while the rich white chocolate ice cream seasoned with sake and ginger cleanses the palate of the spicy bite.

The Restaurant at Kellogg Ranch

The Collins School of Hospitality Management, Cal Poly Pomona

3801 West Temple Avenue
Pomona, California 91768
909-869-4700
www.rkr.csupomona.edu

Grilled Lamb and Garlic Sausages, Spring Vegetables, Haricots Flageolets and Herbes de Provence

By Chef Scott Rudolph

Serves 8

INGREDIENTS

Spring Vegetables:
1/4 cup olive oil
8 baby artichokes, trimmed, quartered, cooked
1 cup yellow bell pepper, roasted, large dice
1/4 cup capers, drained, rinsed
1/2 cup nicoise olives, pitted
4 cups baby spinach leaves, washed
1 cup yellow pear tomatoes, halved
1 cup red pear tomatoes, halved
1 cup bacon/pancetta/smoked sausage, cooked, chopped (optional)

1 cup haricot flageolet, cooked
Kosher salt, to taste
Cracked black pepper, to taste
8 links lamb and garlic sausage, grilled, sliced
Sheep's milk cheese, shredded (optional, to taste)
Fresh herbes de Provenance, to taste

Lamb and Garlic Sausage:
2-1/2 lbs lamb shoulder, cubed
2-1/2 lbs lamb loin, medium dice
2 oz kosher salt

1/2 oz dextrose
1/2 oz white pepper, ground
1/4 oz tinted curing mixture
1-1/2 lbs ice, crushed
2-3/4 oz nonfat dry milk powder
1/2 oz herbes de Provence (dried)
1-1/2 lbs garlic cloves, braised, small dice
1-1/4 lbs pork fatback, small dice
12 feet hog casing

PREPARATION INSTRUCTIONS

Spring Vegetables: In a large sauté pan heat olive oil and add ingredients one by one. Sauté quickly (do not overcook tomatoes) and season well. Divide vegetables evenly and place on heated plates. Top vegetables with sliced sausage. Garnish with cheese and herbs. Serve immediately.

Lamb and Garlic Sausage: Mix together salt, dextrose, pepper and tinted curing mixture. Toss the lamb shoulder with half that mix, and chill well. Toss the lamb loin with the remaining half of the mix, chill and reserve. Progressive grind (1/4 – 1/8 inch plates) the chilled lamb shoulder and chill well. Grind the fatback through the 1/8-inch plate and freeze.

In a chilled chopper bowl, add the chilled ground lamb shoulder and crushed ice and process until the mixture rises to 30°F. Add the frozen fat back and process, scraping bowl, until mixture reaches 40°F. Add the nonfat dry milk powder and continue processing until the mixture reaches 58°F.

(cont'd)

ABOUT THE CHEF

Chef Scott Rudolph is a full-time faculty member at The Collins School of Hospitality Management at the California State Polytechnic University, Pomona. He lectures and instructs students in the culinary arts and food and beverage operations at the Restaurant at Kellogg Ranch, the student operated and managed fine dining and banquet facility. He advocates helping students learn how to make ethical, logical, and productive choices and assume responsibility for their own lives. His formal education includes a Master of Arts candidacy in Career and Technical (vocational) Education at the California State University, San Bernardino; a Bachelor of Arts degree in Literature from Point Loma Nazarene University in San Diego, California, and an Associate of Occupational Studies degree in Culinary Arts from The Culinary Institute of America in Hyde Park, New York.

Before joining The Collins School he was Culinary Arts Coordinator/Chef Instructor for Paso Robles Public Schools/Santa Lucia ROP in San Luis Obispo County, California; Academic Chair/Chef Instructor for the California School of Culinary Arts/Le Cordon Bleu North America in Pasadena, California; Executive Chef for ARAMARK Corporation in San Ramon, California; Executive Chef for LSG Sky Chefs in Los Angeles, California; and President/Executive Chef for Coast Cuisine Corporation in San Diego, California. Chef Rudolph lives and participates in the City of Pomona's Arts Colony where he volunteers his time to the City of Pomona and to the students of the Pomona Unified School District.

PREPARATION INSTRUCTIONS
(cont'd)

Transfer mixture to a bowl placed over an ice bath and fold in the chilled diced lamb loin, herbes de Provence, diced garlic and chilled diced fatback. Test the mixture, adjust the seasonings if necessary. Stuff into rinsed casings and twist into 6 inch links.

Poach links in 160°F water to an internal temperature of 150°F and shock in ice water. Dry links well, cover, label, date and refrigerate for up to 1 week.

Place sausages on a clean, well seasoned, hot grill and cook until well colored and heated through, bias slice and hold for service. While sausages are cooking, heat oil in a large sauté pan, make Spring Vegetables. Sauté quickly until vegetables are just heated through and spinach is just wilted, being sure not to overcook the tomatoes. Season

vegetables well and transfer to a heated service platter, arrange sausages on top, garnish with cheese and fresh herbs. Serve immediately.

HELPFUL HINTS, VARIATIONS OR OTHER ADVICE

Pair this dish with a garden salad for a light lunch. Arrange attractively on a platter for family-style service or divide the portions equally for à la carte service.

SUGGESTED WINE PAIRING

- 2001 Guigal Chateauneuf-du-Pape
- 2002 Bogle Petite Sirah California

THE STORY BEHIND THE RECIPE

In the restaurant we try to utilize and highlight as many products as possible from the College of Agriculture. In this dish we use lamb, various pork products and whatever vegetables and herbs are available at the moment. The synergy between various departments on campus and the restaurant is exciting and adds to the experience for both the student and the guest.

Roppongi Restaurant & Sushi Bar

875 Prospect Street
La Jolla, California 92037
858-551-5252
www.roppongiusa.com

Polynesian Crab Stack

By Chef Stephen B. Window

Serves 4-6

INGREDIENTS

Dressing:
6 Tbs fresh ginger, peeled and chopped
4 Tbs sugar
6 Tbs lime juice
2 Tbs garlic, diced
1/2 cup water

Crab Stack:
1/4 cup pea shoots
1/4 cup Roma tomatoes, diced
1/4 cup cucumber, sliced
1/4 cup red onion, diced
1/4 cup mango, diced

1/4 cup avocado, diced
1/4 cup fresh crab meat
2 Tbs peanuts, chopped
1 tsp fresh cilantro, chopped

PREPARATION INSTRUCTIONS

Ginger-Lime Dressing:

Combine ginger with sugar, lime juice, garlic and water. Let sit overnight in refrigerator.

Crab Stack:

With pea shoots at the bottom and crab meat at the top, tightly layer pea shoots, tomatoes, cucumber, onion, mango, avocado and crab into a mold.

Plating:

Invert onto serving plate. Sprinkle plate with chopped peanuts and cilantro. Drizzle with dressing.

HELPFUL HINTS, VARIATIONS OR OTHER ADVICE

Use a cylindrical mold to mold ahead of time.

ABOUT THE CHEF

Executive Chef Window began his training in England where he studied in the classical tradition of London's finest hotels and was a finalist in England's "Young Chef of the Year" competition. His vast culinary experience has taken him to epicurean capitals throughout Europe, Asia and the U.S. Chef Window has been twice honored as "Featured Chef" at the James Beard House in Manhattan, while serving as the driving force behind the innovative, award-winning menu at Roppongi for the past seven years.

SUGGESTED WINE PAIRING

• 2005 Etude Pinot Gris

THE STORY BEHIND THE RECIPE

This recipe has been the #1 selling item at Roppongi for the past seven years. Its Hawaiian and Thai flavors are blended with the fresh, local produce of Southern California. The crab stack is Roppongi's best-selling item because it is refreshing and healthy, with only 350 calories, 15 grams of fat and 45 mg of cholesterol.

Scripps College

1030 Columbia Avenue
Claremont, California 91711
909-607-2977

Double Chocolate Kahlúa Ravioli

By Chef Dale McDonald

Serves 4

INGREDIENTS

Ravioli:
1/4 cup Kahlúa, poured over chopped chocolate
1 1/2 lbs dark chocolate, cut into 1" pieces
2 cups heavy whipping cream
6 won ton wraps (large, egg roll size)
1 cup vegetable oil

White Chocolate Foam:
1-1/2 cups whipping cream
1 lb white chocolate, cut into 1/4-inch pieces
1 cup heavy whipping cream (or whipped topping)
White and dark chocolate shavings
4 sprigs fresh mint leaves

PREPARATION INSTRUCTIONS

Ravioli:

The day before serving, pour Kahlúa over chocolate pieces in medium-size bowl and set aside. Bring the whipping cream to a boil and pour over dark chocolate mixture. Whisk together until mixed then refrigerate overnight. Mixture will harden when chilled.

The next day, place one won ton wrap on work surface. With a melon baller, scoop 4 balls of dark chocolate and place in four corners of wrap. Moisten around balls with water, placing one additional wrap on top. Press gently around chocolate, cut into 4 squares, using a fork to crimp edges. Set aside until all are made. Heat vegetable oil over medium-high heat (minimum 375°F). Place ravioli in oil until golden brown (about 1 to 1-1/2 minutes).

White Chocolate Foam:

Boil heavy whipping cream and pour over white chocolate. Whisk until mixed and let cool. Place 1 cup whipping cream in mixer, turn on high. When cream starts to set, add 1 cup of white chocolate cream mixture; reserve remainder for garnish. Mix only until soft peaks begin to form, set aside.

Plating:

Assemble 3 warm ravioli on large plate with white chocolate foam and sprinkle with shaved white and dark chocolate and mint sprigs.

HELPFUL HINTS, VARIATIONS OR OTHER ADVICE

Drizzle remaining white chocolate cream sauce over the raviolis for added sweetness. Chef recommends using high quality Swiss Chalet Ultra White Chocolate.

ABOUT THE CHEF

Chef Dale McDonald started his career working at a bakery called Pastries by Kathi, working his way up to making all the pastries and cakes as well as being in charge of the restaurant. He then went to college at the New England Culinary Institute in Essex, Vermont. From there he went on to the Ritz Carlton Resort in Rancho Mirage, California, working as an assistant to the Pastry Chef. After that he went to work at the Queen Mary in Long Beach, California as the Garde-Manger Chef. After his time at the Queen, he went on to design and open several restaurants as the Executive Chef including Cafe 37, Cafe Tirol and Omas European Restaurant and Bakery. He decided to move back to the desert and became the Chef de Partie at the Renaissance Esmeralda Resort in Indian Wells, California. He soon went on to be the Country Club Chef at the Marriott Rancho Las Palmas Resort and Spa in Rancho Mirage, California. Now he is an Executive Chef with Sodexho at Scripps College in Claremont, California.

Skimmer's Panini Grill

25290 Marguerite Parkway, Suite E
Mission Viejo, California 92692
949-855-8500

The Houston Panini Sandwich

By Chef Scott K. Kim

Serves 4

INGREDIENTS

8 slices thin cut sourdough bread
1 cup Skimmer's Chipotle Lime Mayo (recipe below)
8 oz Gruyère, shredded
16 oz roast beef, sliced
4 Tbs Ortega green chiles
Kosher salt, to taste

Skimmer's Chipotle Lime Mayo:

1 bunch green onion, chopped
1/2 bunch cilantro, chopped
6 oz prepared chipotle in adobo, puréed
2 qts Best Foods mayo
1 cup fresh lime juice
1 Tbs Tabasco sauce
1 Tbs kosher salt, to taste

PREPARATION INSTRUCTIONS

Chipotle Lime Mayo:

Combine all ingredients. Mix thoroughly and check seasonings to taste.

Panini:

Spread Skimmer's Chipotle Lime Mayo liberally on two slices of the bread. Working on one side, spread gruyere evenly over mayo. Arrange roast beef evenly over gruyere. Sprinkle on Ortega chiles. Adjust seasoning with kosher salt. Cover with other piece of bread to form sandwich. Grill on sandwich press until crispy and golden on the outside and hot and melted on the inside.

HELPFUL HINTS, VARIATIONS OR OTHER ADVICE

Avoid touching face when working with chipotles. Wash hands after handling. Sandwich will be better if weighted or pressed while grilling or baking. Results are best if you use high quality ingredients. Instead of using a sandwich press, you can bake the sandwich in an oven at 300°F, just make sure you flip it once.

ABOUT THE CHEF

Scott K. Kim began cooking to put himself through college at the University of California, Riverside in 1985 where he earned a B.A. in Psychology. He fell in love with the food industry through restaurant work and catering and attended the Culinary Institute of America, New York in 1988. After 10 years in sales and sales management in the wine and liquor industry, Scott opened Skimmer's in Mission Viejo in 2003. Skimmer's has a successful catering department and will begin serving breakfast by the end of 2006.

SUGGESTED WINE PAIRING

- This sandwich is great a with medium-bodied red like a Shiraz, a Merlot or a Zinfandel. I like the current vintage of Grgich Hills Zinfandel. Also, this is excellent with an imported beer such as Heineken or Sapporo.

THE STORY BEHIND THE RECIPE

I wanted to have a sandwich on the Skimmer's menu with a little kick! The Houston is one of our top selling sandwiches.

Spazio Restaurant

14755 Ventura Boulevard
Sherman Oaks, California 91403
818-728-8400
www.spazio.la

Chicken Breast and Shrimp with Provençal Herbs in Pistachio Dijonnaise Sauce

By Chef Eli Bernard Tordjman

Serves 4

INGREDIENTS

2 Tbs butter
2 Tbs olive oil
8 (U/10-12) shrimp
4 chicken breasts, 8 oz each, skinless and boneless
Salt and pepper, to taste
1 cup dry wine
1 cup chicken stock
1 shallot
2 cloves garlic

Sauce:
1 cup cream
1/2 Tbs Dijon mustard
Few drops lemon juice
2 Tbs herbes de Provence (tarragon, dill, basil, thyme)
2 Tbs pistachio nuts

PREPARATION INSTRUCTIONS

Shrimp and Chicken:

Heat the butter and the olive oil in a sauté pan. Add the shrimp and sauté over high heat, stirring occasionally until the shrimp turn pink (about 2-3 minutes). Remove and set on a plate. Season the chicken with salt and pepper and add them to the pan over medium heat for 3-4 minutes each side. Add the wine, then the chicken stock, let cook for another 6-8 minutes each side. Add shallots and garlic, letting them fall to the bottom of the pan until they are tender but not browned. Remove the chicken and set aside on a plate.

Sauce:

Using the same pan, add cream, mustard and a few drops of lemon. Add the herbes de provence and stir all together. Remove pan from heat. Peel shells off shrimp, leaving them intact. Transfer shrimp to a bowl. Return sauce to heat, bring to a boil and simmer until thickened slightly, 2-3 minutes. Return chicken and shrimp to pan and reheat for 1-2 minutes.

Garnish:

Sprinkle with pistachio nuts.

ABOUT THE CHEF

Eli Bernard Tordjman has been the Executive Chef at Spazio restaurant, Sherman Oaks, CA since 1999. He was born December 21, 1935 in Versailles, France. He was educated as a Master Chef at Le Votre Restaurant Academy, Versailles from 1974-1976. He was the Executive Chef at Ma Maison, Denver, CO from 1984-1990; the Head Chef and Catering Manager at Le Château, Paris from 1991 to 1994; Executive Chef, Café Noir, San Pedro, CA from 1994 to 1998; Signature Grill, Sherman Oaks, CA from 1998 to 1999, and Bagatelle Restaurant, Los Angeles, CA from 2001 to present. He has been reviewed in several publications such as the *Los Angelas Times* (1998) and the *Daily News* (2000) and has also been on TV and radio for KNEW in Denver and Talk Radio 97.1.

Spotlight Café

1622 19th Street
Bakersfield, California 93301
661-634-0692
www.spotlighttheatreandcafe.com

Cream of Kern Soup

By Chef David Jones

Serves 8

INGREDIENTS

6 carrots, peeled and cut into 2" pieces
2 onions, peeled and cut into 2" pieces
7 cloves garlic, peeled
2 Tbs olive oil
4 Tbs butter
1/4 cup flour
2 cups heavy cream

1 liter bottle Bolthouse Farms™ Carrot Juice
1 tsp pepper
1 tsp salt
1/2 tsp thyme
1/4 cup sour cream
14 cup cilantro leaves
1/4 cup sliced almonds

PREPARATION INSTRUCTIONS

Preheat oven to 350°F. Drizzle oil over carrots, onion and garlic. Reserve one clove garlic for garnish. Bake for one hour at 350°F, stirring occasionally until tender. Melt butter in sauce pan, add flour to make a roux and slowly add one cup heavy cream stirring constantly. When thickened, add remaining cream. Purée baked vegetables with 1/2 bottle of carrot juice, leaving some texture. Pour purée mixture into pan. Add remaining juice and seasonings. Simmer on low until creamy and flavors blend.

Garnish:
Serve with drizzle of sour cream, garnish with fresh cilantro and chopped roasted almonds.

HELPFUL HINTS, VARIATIONS OR OTHER ADVICE

Garnish with fresh sliced avocado and a dollop of cremé fresh.

ABOUT THE CHEF

Executive Chef David Jones was born and raised in Connecticut. After marrying and moving to California, he realized his love for cooking and returned to Connecticut to receive his training at the Center For Culinary Arts. After graduating, Chef Jones returned to Bakersfield, California where he catered small events on his own. In 2004, Spotlight Café offered him a position in the kitchen. Since then he was promoted to Executive Chef where he has been instrumental in the expansion and development of the café's daily menu and catering services. He brings ideas that are outside the box, healthy and just taste great.

THE STORY BEHIND THE RECIPE

This recipe was created when a local magazine called for recipes made only with products from Kern County. The ingredients, including the Bolthouse Farms juice, are all grown or produced in Kern County, California. Our Cream of Kern was the featured soup in the resulting article. We posted the recipe and article on our webpage and many of our customers expressed delight in preparing it themselves.

Tam O' Shanter Inn

2980 Los Feliz Boulevard
Los Angeles, California 90039
323-664-0228
www.lawrysonline.com

Toad in the Hole

By Chef Oscar Pacheco

Serves 4

INGREDIENTS

Brown gravy mix
1-1/2 cups water
1/4 cup Burgundy wine
4 Tbs butter, melted
1 large onion, coarsely chopped
3/4 medium green pepper, coarsely chopped
1/2 lb small fresh mushrooms, washed, leave stems on
1 lb filet mignon, cubed
Lawry's Seasoned Salt, to taste
Lawry's Seasoned Pepper, to taste

Yorkshire Pudding:
1 cup less 1 teaspoon flour
1/2 tsp salt
2 eggs, beaten
1 cup milk
Cooking oil

PREPARATION INSTRUCTIONS

Combine brown gravy mix, water and wine. Bring to a boil. Reduce heat and simmer uncovered for 5 to 7 minutes. Set aside and keep warm. Sauté vegetables in 2 Tbs butter and season to taste. Set aside and keep warm. Sauté filet pieces in 2 Tbs butter. Season to taste. Place filet pieces in each Yorkshire shell. Cover each with vegetables and spoon brown gravy over all.

Yorkshire Pudding Shell:

Sift together flour and salt. Make a well and add beaten eggs. Blend. Add milk, beating continuously for 10 minutes. Let stand 1 hour. Heat oven to 450°F. Place 5-inch omelet pan in oven to heat. When hot, coat pan with oil and heat again. Pour 1/2 cup batter into pan, bake for 35 minutes. Repeat with remaining batter.

ABOUT THE CHEF
Oscar Pacheco is the Executive Chef at the Tam O'Shanter Restaurant. He has been with Lawry's restaurants since 1994. Oscar trained at Lawry's in Las Vegas and helped open Lawry's in Taipei. Oscar has studied in various culinary institutes and continues his training here at Tam O' Shanter.

UC Santa Cruz Dining Services

1156 High Street
Santa Cruz, California 95064
831-459-4612
housing.ucsc.edu/dining/index.html

CALIFORNIA
Restaurant
ASSOCIATION
CELEBRATING 100 YEARS OF SERVICE
1906·2006

Sesame-Grilled Mahi Mahi with Mango Macadamia Pesto

By Chef Dwight Collins, CEC

Serves 6

INGREDIENTS

Mango Macadamia Pesto:
1 cup fresh mango, medium dice
1/4 cup fresh basil leaves, packed
2 cloves fresh garlic
1/2 cup extra virgin olive oil
1/2 cup toasted macadamia nuts
6 fresh mint leaves
1 Tbs Jamaican jerk seasoning
1 tsp kosher salt (or to taste)
1 tsp brown sugar

Sesame Grilled Mahi Mahi:
1/2 cup vegetable oil
1/4 cup sesame oil
1/4 cup frozen orange juice concentrate, undiluted
6 black peppercorns, crushed
1/2 tsp ground white pepper
2 tsp Kikkoman soy sauce
3 lb Mahi Mahi fillets, skin off, cut 6-8 oz.

PREPARATION INSTRUCTIONS

Pesto:
Combine Mango Macadamia Pesto ingredients in a food processor or blender and pulse until chunky. Do not liquefy. Set aside.

Mahi Mahi:
Combine Mahi marinade ingredients, pour over the fillets and marinate for 1 to 2 hours. Remove fillets from marinade and grill until fish flakes when pierced with a fork.

Plating:
Serve topped with Mango Macadamia Pesto.

HELPFUL HINTS, VARIATIONS OR OTHER ADVICE

Adjust salt and brown sugar levels to personal preference.

ABOUT THE CHEF

Dwight Collins has 32 years experience in food service, ranging from opening B&I accounts in the Silicon Valley (Intel, Amdahl, Raychem, Oracle, etc.) to opening and operating restaurants in Carson City, Nevada: Sanderlings at Seascape Resort, the National Steinbeck Center, Pajaro Dunes on Monterey Bay, and currently at UC Santa Cruz as campus Executive Chef. His clam chowder recipe has won six times at the Santa Cruz Beach Boardwalk competition, and earlier this month his BBQ sauce recipe took 1st place at the Autry Museum BBQ competition in Los Angeles. He was certified by the American Culinary Federation as Certified Executive Chef in 1992, and serves on the Chef's Council of the Center for Culinary Development in San Francisco (ccdsf.com).

SUGGESTED WINE PAIRING

• 2004 Morgan Sauvignon Blanc

THE STORY BEHIND THE RECIPE

I developed this recipe after catching a 40-pound Dorado in Akumal, Mexico, and fed the boat crew's family and friends with it (instead of mint, which wasn't available, I used, ever present in Mexico, cilantro).

California Restaurant Association Educational Foundation

The California Restaurant Association Educational Foundation (CRAEF) seeks to promote both the hospitality industry throughout California and its educational system as a career of pride and professionalism, to strengthen training and educational preparation for hospitality careers, and to encourage able students to seek such careers.

California Restaurant Association

The California Restaurant Association, now celebrating its 100th year of service, is the definitive voice of the California restaurant and hospitality industry. The restaurant industry is the largest private employer in California, representing nearly 1.4 million jobs. Restaurants produce more than $51 billion In sales annually and generate more than $4 billion in sales tax for the state.

Western Foodservice & Hospitality Expo

More than 15,000 foodservice professionals from every segment of the industry attend the annual Western Foodservice & Hospitality Expo to search for new food, hot trends, innovative products and new suppliers among the 600+ exhibitors. Exciting features include the Los Angeles Wine and Food Festival, Ultimate Barista Challenge, Pizza Pavilion and Competitions, new product tastings and international sampling. The Expo is sponsored by the California Restaurant Association and produced and managed by Reed Exhibitions.

Los Angeles Wine & Food Festival

Three days when Wine Country makes its home in Los Angeles. The Los Angeles Wine & Food Festival allows consumers and the professional trade to explore, sample and expand their knowledge of wine as they stroll among hundreds of wineries – all within tasting distance of one another. Also, it is the opportunity to discover foods that pair well with wine as well as every conceivable wine accessory available. Exciting event features include a Reserve Wine & Food Tasting, celebrity chef demonstrations, and a Chocolate Tasting Corner. The Festival is produced and managed by Reed Exhibitions, World of Wines, LLC, and The Monterey Wine Festival.